# A Fish Made of Water

*An Oracle's Guide to the Spiritual Universe*

MICHAEL OLIN-HITT, PH.D.

*Braided Way Media*

*To Jennifer, my spiritual companion
and beloved wife.*

Published by
Braided Way Media, LLC
2326 Cheviot Hills Ln.
Vandalia, OH 45377

ISBN 978-0-9835428-0-3

**Library of Congress Cataloging-in-Publication Data**

Olin-Hitt, Michael
A Fish Made of Water: An Oracle's Guide to the Spiritual Universe
Michael Olin-Hitt
p.   cm.
ISBN 978-0-9835428-0-3
Library of Congress Control Number: 2011927571

1. Channeling.   2. Metaphysical   I. Title

Printed in the USA

Cover image by Terry K. Hitt

# Table of Contents

# Introduction

IKE MOST PEOPLE, MY LIFE is comprised of several roles. By day, I am an English Professor. At home, I am husband and father. At church, I am the pastor's spouse. But I have one role that is unusual and difficult to explain. I am an oracle.

Since 1998, I have been able to enter into an altered state of consciousness or trance, during which a spiritual presence speaks through me. The result is astounding information that is far beyond my knowledge. The spiritual messenger who speaks through me has never given me a name and has said simply, "I am of the Holy." So, I have called this guide "the Messenger of the Holy," or "the Messenger" for short.

In our culture, the two most prominent terms to describe my experience would be "deep-trance channeling" and "prophecy." Given the options of calling myself a channel or a prophet, I have gravitated instead toward the ancient term of "oracle," a choice I shall explain shortly.

Here is how I experience what I call the oracle state. I invite the experience by focusing on light and goodness, which I symbolize by lighting a candle. I then open my mind to the Sacred through meditation and prayer. After I center my thoughts on Holiness, I begin to feel spiritual energy course through my body. Often, I have short vocal outbursts of "Ha," which my wife jokingly calls spiritual Tourettes.

At this point, I can stop the process, but if I decide to surrender, I feel a spiritual energy seep into my chest and rise into my throat. First, I lose control of my breathing, which becomes deep. Then I feel my throat tense, as if a power has entered me and seized my vocal chords. Finally, I lose control of my body and enter into a mystical state of awareness. My eyes close. I sometimes tremble. After several long breaths, words pour forth from my lips.

I hear the messages as they come through me, and I receive mental images that correlate with the words, but until the message is over, I cannot move my body or speak my own thoughts. In fact, my mind becomes dormant, and I simply listen as the messages unfold.

## The Channel, The Prophet, The Shaman and The Oracle

Human beings have had this type of mystical connection to the Sacred since the dawn of human awareness, and it has been understood and explained by various religious and cultural frameworks. It is the experience of the shaman, or the words of the prophet, or the advice of the oracle, or the guidance of the channel. In today's culture, I found that there is no "safe" way to identify spiritual gifts without aligning to very specific sub-groups. Our world is one that is divided by lines of religious dogmas. Most people of our time understand my experience as deep-trance channeling. While channeling is a very accurate way to describe my experience, I have avoided using this term to identify my gift. First of all, the term "channeling" is associated not only with the process of receiving inspired messages, but also with the content of the messages. In today's culture, channeling is dominated by messages about self-help through positive thinking, and the messages I receive deviate from this contemporary trend. Second, I find that the word "channeling" causes emotional aversion to people in traditional faith communities, and I want to be accessible to people of all traditions, or no tradition.

When I first began to receive messages from spiritual guides, I gravitated toward the word "prophecy" to describe the experience. I liked the association of prophecy with ancient spiritual traditions. With research, I found that the experience of falling into a trance and speaking spiritual guidance is indeed one of the prominent forms of biblical prophecy. However, in contemporary culture prophecy is misunderstood and is limited to predictions of the end times, and I found that using the term caused misunderstandings both within and outside the Christian community. On a humorous note, I also had to acknowledge that prophets have a historically limited life-expectancy, and I didn't want to place myself into direct conflict with groups that may wish to stone me. So, through a few hard knocks, I learned to avoid the term "prophecy."

I also avoided the role of the shaman. I admire and appreciate indigenous forms of religion, but finally, I can't claim alignment with shamanic traditions, so I thought the shamanic terminology was outside of my reach. In addition, vocalizing spiritual wisdom from an altered state of consciousness is only one of many gifts of the shaman.

Finally, I became comfortable with the term "oracle." In ancient Greece and Rome, an oracle was a person who often entered an altered state of awareness to give voice to guidance and predictions from the Gods. Of all the terms to describe my sacred experience, "oracle" is the most neutral in our current culture. There is a great deal of mystery surrounding the Greek and Roman oracles of old, and I would rather align myself with mystery than with misunderstanding. In addition, the role I serve for people is closely aligned with the roles of the ancient oracles. People come to me to receive the Messenger's guidance and advice on a variety of topics, from the personal to the political, and from the spiritual to the physical, which was true for the Greek and Roman oracles as well.

It has always been my intention to work with people of all faith traditions or no faith tradition, and aligning my gift with that of the oracle has allowed me to do this. People of almost all faith orientations understand the word "oracle" without deep, emotional associations. There is another benefit to the word "oracle" because it has three possible meanings. It can be the person who receives the sacred message, the place where the message is received—such as the Oracle of Delphi—or it can also describe the message itself. Thus, in this book, I am an oracle (one who receives a message) presenting oracles (or spiritual messages) for our time.

Some scholars postulate that the Oracle of Delphi would sit over a fault line in the earth, from which gasses would emanate into the temple. These gasses, it is thought, caused the altered state of consciousness for the oracle. However, based on my experience, no external substances, such as gasses, are needed to reach the trance state that allows an oracle to emerge. For some reason unknown to me, a small group of people are constructed in such a way to allow for quick entry into a trance state, through which spiritual communication is possible. I happen to be one of those people. It was not a gift I asked for or even understood as it began. The oracle experience merely came upon me in 1998 as I took prayer seriously in my own spiritual journey.

## Wisdom Sessions and the Origins of This Book

It did not take long for me to realize that an oracle gift is wasted unless it is shared. For over ten years, I have shared this gift with people during what I call "wisdom sessions." People come to these sessions to receive spiritual advice and guidance, and I have witnessed lives changed as a result. People's spiritual journeys have deepened. Spiritual awareness has become heightened. Relationships have been healed. On several occasions there have been physical healings.

I usually conduct wisdom sessions with groups of up to 10 people, and the pattern of the sessions has always been the same. Once I enter the oracle state, there is a general lesson for the group, which often addresses topics such as the origins of the soul, the purpose of physical life, the nature and flow of spiritual energy, or the presence of spiritual messengers. After this general lesson, each person receives an individual message, which addresses personal issues I could not know about. A wisdom session lasts up to two hours, during which I am in a trance the entire time. I am beyond being surprised at the miraculous guidance which comes during wisdom sessions, but I am always amazed. It is a humbling experience to be a vessel for holy work.

Over the years, I have been astounded at the beauty, truth and depth of the general messages of the wisdom sessions. I decided that I could compile these lessons into a book. The problem was that the book would be patched together from numerous wisdom sessions. Then it occurred to a friend that we should have wisdom sessions for the expressed purpose of receiving a book. Why not let the Messenger of the Holy dictate the book in extended sessions? We formed a "book group" of people who wanted to enter into wisdom sessions to receive general messages appropriate for a larger audience. We met once a month, and this book is a result of these wisdom sessions. The wisdom sessions were recorded, then transcribed by a loving friend. I then took the transcriptions and edited them for a general audience. A single session would last up to 3 hours and produce over 20 pages of single-spaced transcription, so I had to make some choices about what to include.

Even with editing, the messages are not totally linear. Channeled material, or in this case oracle material, is often very dense and circuitous. Many readers will find it necessary to read short sections of the messages at a time. Most of the chapters end with a question and answer section, in which my friends in the book group dialogued with the Messenger.

## Contemporary Messages of Ancient Wisdom

What you will find in this book is a new and fresh perspective and terminology to understand the spiritual universe. There are oracles (or messages) about the origins of the universe, the purpose of our souls, our role in the Holy Design, and ways to increase our sacred awareness.

What has fascinated me over the years is that the messages that come during wisdom sessions are aligned with the wisdom of the world's ancient religions. Because of my oracular experiences, I have been drawn to the scriptures of world traditions, and I continue to stumble over the very ideas and guidance that have been spoken through me during wisdom sessions. This leads me to believe that there is a deep mysticism, which links our many faith traditions through essential truths. While the messages that come through me have resonance with ancient wisdom traditions, the messages also have a contemporary framework because of the influences my language and background have upon the messages.

Inspired wisdom—from the prophet, channel or oracle—is always a combination of spiritual material framed in the language and cultural understanding of the one who receives the message. For this reason, spiritual messages are always limited by human perspective. In the Genesis creation story of the seven days, for instance, the world is presented as flat with an arched "firmament" separating the waters of heaven from the waters below. In other words, the flat earth is completely surrounded by waters. The deep, sacred truth of the story is framed in the historical, human understanding of the universe, dated around 586 B.C.

In our present age, our understanding of the universe has changed rapidly over the past two centuries; however, our sacred texts still reflect pre-enlightenment cosmology. As a result, the spiritual truths of our faith traditions do not reflect our common understanding of the universe.

It is time for a contemporary framework for spiritual truth. I am not suggesting that we reject the scriptures of our rich faith traditions, but I do believe we are in need of updated spiritual guidance for the very real challenges of our time.

The reason I decided to write this book is because I believe the oracles I receive are essential to create spiritual orientation for our age. From the beginning of my oracular experiences, I have been introduced to a new terminology and framework to describe the spiritual universe. As a result, sacred wisdom has been communicated in fresh and contemporary concepts.

The terminology of this book invites people of all faith orientations into a common perspective. Therefore, the spiritual universe presented in this book can allow for a healing of the deep religious divisions in our world. In the terminology of this book, all faith traditions and concepts of God are honored. The Messenger of the Holy presents a concept for God that includes but transcends our ideas of a personal God. For this all-encompassing concept of God, the words "the Holy Whole" or "the Sacred All" are used. For the many elements of the

Sacred—including the spiritual energy that courses through all life—the Messenger of the Holy uses the term "the Holy." Through this neutral terminology and through the broad spiritual perspective of the oracles in this book, you will be able to understand the spiritual universe in contemporary concepts and see your place in this universe with clarity and purpose.

## The Braided Way: Toward a Universal Spirituality

In chapter three, entitled "The Braided Way," the Messenger of the Holy presents a means to view all sacred traditions as interrelated. In this wisdom session, we are invited to view each faith tradition as a strand that is woven into one, large braid of Truth. Each strand adds to the strength of the braid, and the braid is weakened whenever any strand, or religious tradition, is ignored or severed. The metaphor of the sacred braid allows us to see the value of combining faith traditions in order to have a more complete awareness of the sacred mystery of the universe. Throughout human history, we have been divided by our religions, but in the Braided Way, we see the wisdom of understanding that each faith tradition offers a valuable perspective that strengthens our over-all view of the Sacred.

Central to the Braided Way is the idea of the Holy Whole. In the Holy Whole, the Messenger provides an expansive concept for the Sacred, in which all of our concepts of God are embraced. The Holy Whole represents the unity of the Sacred, and in this unity, each faith tradition offers a valuable but limited view of the Whole. Thus, to better understand the mystery of the Holy Whole, we should embrace, not shun, the variety of expressions of Sacred awareness. In the Holy Whole the idea that God is singular is reflected in the Wholeness of the Sacred. At the same time, the idea that God is multiple is reflected in the innumerable parts of the Holy Whole. The concept that God is a personality is embraced as well as the idea that there is only Universal Consciousness without personality. The awareness that the Spirit infuses all things, including the Earth, is also reflected in the wholeness of the universe. In the Holy Whole, the Sacred is both immanent and transcendent, both beyond and within.

Since the totality of the Holy is beyond our comprehension, we must realize that any single presentation of God is limited. In the Braided Way, we are invited to combine these multiple perspectives in order to come closer to an awareness of the Whole.

Of all the lessons I have received, the idea of the Braided Way propelled me to write this book. Many people today invite the multiple perspectives of our faith traditions into their lives, but there are no frameworks that allow us to combine these faith traditions into a greater Whole. The Braided Way gives us permission to encounter the Sacred through many traditions, and it allows us to celebrate the religious diversity of our world.

The Braided Way also provides the foundation for this book because the lessons from the wisdom sessions are reflective of so many of our faith traditions. In a sense, this book is an example of the Braided Way in action.

## Channeling and The New Age Tradition

While the lessons that I receive are reflective of the deep wisdom of many faith traditions, any follower of a specific tradition will find deviations from their religious dogmas. Thus, readers of this book will need to be willing to encounter ideas that are not in total alignment with any single religious tradition.

This is ironically true even of the "New Age" or "New Thought" movement, which is the contemporary tradition most open to channeled material. Calling the New Age movement a "tradition" may be overstepping the intent of those who read the contemporary books that combine spirituality with self help. However, there are dominating trends in these works, most notably the emphasis on our thoughts manifesting in our reality, in either positive ways (such as prosperity) or negative ways (such as disease). While the messages that come through me are in alignment with many of the New Age ideas — such as the divinity within, the flow of spiritual energy, the work of spiritual messengers and the power of spiritual healing — the idea that our thoughts directly manifest into our reality in tangible and material ways is absent in this book. This difference from popular trends deserves note because a great deal of the "law of attraction" movement has come about because of channeled material, first through Jane Roberts in the Seth books, then through Esther Hicks in the Abraham books.

This book is channeled material of a different nature.

You will not find guidance in this book to make the law of attraction work for you, but you may find insights which explain why this approach does *not* work for you. In the spiritual universe described in this book, thoughts have an *influence* over our health and our perception of reality, but reality itself is comprised of a complex web of interrelated elements, making our lives only an influence of many influences. What this book will do is help you learn to be a sacred influence within the mysterious web of life.

In this book, we are invited into the wonder and fulfillment of knowing that we are connected to all things through both Spirit and matter. In this book, we are taught that the essential Self, the core of our being, is Sacred. In other words, we contain a spark from the origins of the universe. We are taught that the way to the Sacred is through the Self. And we are given a perspective which allows us to see the purpose of our soul in the Grand Design of creation. Most of all, we are taught how to honor and respect all of our faith traditions and all of creation during a time in our collective history in which these lessons could save our civilization and our planet.

In this book, I invite you on a journey into holy awareness in which you will see the ancient become new and in which all things are unified into the wholeness of the Sacred.

Peace for the journey,
Michael

## CHAPTER 1

# Fish of Water, Stars in Light: Introductions of Identity

*Note: On January 18, 2010, a group of friends gathered with me for a wisdom session, during which I went into a trance state to allow the spiritual guide we call "the Messenger of the Holy" to speak through me. The purpose of the wisdom session was to receive spiritual guidance that would be gathered into this book. Before the wisdom session, the group talked for a while about the need of our culture for a contemporary description of the spiritual universe. I then lit a candle, and we symbolically purified ourselves with the smoke of burning sage. During the transition into the trance I call the "oracle state," I usually feel vulnerable and self-conscious, so I asked a friend to read sacred texts until the Messenger of the Holy began speaking through me. The Messenger almost always begins with the words, "My children, I see you." On this occasion, my friend read from a book of parallel sayings from Jesus, Buddha, Krishna and Lau Tzu. While focusing on these sayings, I relaxed into the oracle state. The following is a transcript of the words that were spoken through me.*

MY CHILDREN, I see you. I see you. I see you. We are aware of the purpose of your gathering. So, you have brought your souls to magnify and expand the presence of the Holy. You have brought your concerns, your minds, your experiences. You have brought your very lifetimes. You honor us with your presence and your purpose.

Let us begin with introductions. We are of the Holy. We shall not give a name, for a name denotes individual identity, and in the Holy, there is no individuality as you understand it. In the Holy, we cannot distinguish where we end and the rest of the Holy begins. We are as fish of water in the water, fish made of water in the water, spirits made of spirit in the Spirit.

Though there is no distinct individuality in the Holy, there is purpose, which distinguishes us as parts of a greater whole. Our specific purposes are to teach, guide and heal, and in the Holy we merge together as a group. When Michael makes himself available, we merge with him. We utilize his mind, his language and his voice for holy revelation. As a group, various elements of us come to Michael for specific lessons. You may think of us as a hand with fingers. At any given time a single finger may come into Michael for communication, but the entire hand may also enter him to bring images, inspiration and sacred perspective. It is possible to say, then, that the hand of the Holy is upon this one.

As a group, then, we come to you with a unified purpose and intention, and because we come as a singular voice through Michael, we shall use the singular pronoun "I" to identify ourselves. This will allow our voice to be more personal.

So, I shall come to a more simplistic introduction: I—this voice—am a representative and conduit of the Holy. My purpose is to teach, guide and heal, and I am part of a group, which abides in the wholeness of the Holy.

Such is a glimpse of the way we are grouped and abide in the Holy. I tell you, my children, you are no different.

Your individuality is an illusion based upon the perception of your body. But you are not separate from all the rest that is. Indeed, you are all fish of water in the water. You are all spirits of spirit in the Spirit. And so, you are all connected to one another. You are connected to all things. You are connected to the Holy. In your essence, you are spirit, and when you come together in prayer and meditation, I see your spirits merge and blend. In such moments, your awareness expands beyond your physical margins and you glimpse the infinite scope of the Holy.

So, my children, allow me to introduce you to yourselves so that you will know that your Self, your Essence, is of the Holy, connected to the Holy and connected to all things. In the lessons that come through Michael you will see yourself in relationship to the Holy, and you will know your purpose within the Grand Design of creation. In this way, you will become oriented in the spiritual universe. For I tell you, the people are disoriented, unable to see themselves in relationship to the Holy, unable to know that the Sacred resonates in them. It is time for a holy orientation, indeed.

## The Nature of Spiritual Inspiration and Channeled Material

My children, you must understand the nature of divine inspiration so that you will understand both the possibilities and the limitations of these lessons, as well as for all other inspired texts. The voice of God is a voice of no sound. The word of God is a word of no language. How can a voice of no sound and a word of no language come to the people for teaching and guidance? The voice and word must be embodied, and such are the roles of oracles, prophets and channels. These are people who lend their language, thoughts and constructs of understanding to the Holy, and in the merging of the messengers of the Holy with the host, there is both possibility and limitation. Such is the nature of incarnation.

Messengers of the Holy enter into the body, mind and soul of the oracle or prophet. We utilize the conceptual frameworks of the host to compose lessons for guidance and inspiration. But how can the mystery of the Holy, which is beyond your comprehension to understand and your language to describe, be communicated in voice and word? Herein lies the limitation. So, we come and we utilize your language, your concepts, your structure of understanding to communicate that which is beyond your language and your concepts of understandings. So, we will speak in the language of your time and take you to the limits of your abilities to know. And I tell you, there are times when you must *feel* the meanings of the Sacred. The Sacred is beyond your rational thought, so I invite you to become non-rational with me and to *feel* your connection to the Sacred.

So, it has always been that the Holy has come to the people through inspiration, to guide, to heal, to enlighten. Always, the Sacred has chosen to be embodied in language, in art, in life, in movement, in ceremony, in gatherings. But you must understand, my children, that what you know, what you understand, what you hear, what you read is only a minute part of the grandeur of the Holy. For the Holy cannot be captured. The Holy cannot be ensnared. The Holy cannot be described. The Holy cannot be entirely experienced given the limitations of your temporal living.

So, know, my children, that your inspirations, though fulfilling, are partial. Know that the words that describe the Holy are life giving but not complete. So, come with me, and I shall reveal a glimpse of the Sacred, so you may know your place in the Holy, so you may understand the Grand Design and your purpose within the Sacred. Come, and I shall give you a glimpse of the Holy Whole, and in the glimpse may you find fulfillment. May you find direction. May you find peace. May your relationship to the Holy be enhanced.

## The Evolution of Human Consciousness and Sacred Awareness

Bring your minds and your understandings and allow the Sacred to use them and mold them into an awareness of the Holy, and know that inspiration comes to your people in this time. It is not necessary, my children, to limit revelation to the ancient times and languages, for to do so is to limit the ability of the Sacred to grow with you and through you. For I tell you, as human awareness changes so does your ability to understand the Holy. So, the awareness of humanity has expanded. The awareness of humanity has shifted. And yet the language for the Sacred has become dormant. It has caused a great disorientation among the people. Why limit revelation to an ancient language and perspective when revelations come to your time, your place, your people, your situation? This is not to say you should ignore the ancient wisdom of scripture, for the ancient wisdom is true and eternal. However, the eternal wisdom of the Holy must be clothed in the language of the age, and it comes to you now clothed anew in the garments of your time.

So, be open for the inspired revelations of the Holy among you, in you, through you. For the Holy waits to communicate. The Holy waits to inspire. The Holy waits to heal. The Holy waits to be with you. Invite the Holy, then, into your awareness, into your temporal experience, and know that in so doing you invite the Holy to transform your moments of being into more than the temporal can yield. The eternal shall come to the temporal and shall make of your moments revelations of the Sacred. Indeed.

I tell you, humanity is coming to an expanded awareness of the Holy, and this expanded awareness can bring the people to unity in a time of great threat and danger to the divine order of creation. So, the time for renewed and expanded awareness of the Holy is at hand, and we gather for the task.

## A Map of the Holy

My children, an example is in order. Allow me to provide you with sacred perspective by revealing a map of the Holy, and this map will utilize the perception of your age.

In the human experience, mapping is tracing where one has been in order to know how one shall return, but one does not map the Holy. The Holy *reveals* a mapping. The Holy Whole is not of your experience, yet it is reflective of your experience. The Holy Whole is not of your world, yet it is reflected in your world. So, then, I shall utilize the world, your experience, to map the heavens, what I know as the Holy Whole.

To present the heavens, many metaphors have been used. Family systems are used: fathers, sons, mothers. Balances within paradoxes are used: pairings of sky and earth or yin and yang. Architecture is used: palaces, courtyards, thrones, mansions. All are accurate, but all are partial, for the Holy Whole is beyond your minds to conceive and your language to describe.

Is the human understanding and vision not cosmic now? I shall use the cosmos to provide a map of the Holy so you may know your place in the Holy Whole. I shall begin with what you know, then I shall gradually bring you to a new awareness. Let us begin with the stars in order to describe the Holy Whole. Generations have looked to the stars, generations have mapped the stars; but let us not speak of the actual stars, let us speak of the lights of holiness shining as stars in the Holy Whole.

There are lights beyond numbers, all abiding in the Holy Whole. These points of light are gathered in groupings, like constellations and galaxies in your night sky. The human consciousness now understands that the universe expands and moves, and I tell you there are motions also in the Holy Whole. The lights are not stagnant. See in your mind's eye a night sky in which the stars move, merge and journey. And imagine looking into a telescope to see that what looked like a single star to your naked eye is actually a grouping of stars, whose lights have blended together.

But I tell you, the lights of the Holy Whole are not distant. They surround you, even journey through you. So, imagine the starry sky descending upon you so that the lights surround you.

And behold, the night sky itself becomes as light as day. The sky and all around you becomes a field of light, until you can no longer see the individual lights at all. Now imagine that your own body becomes light, so as to be indistinguishable from the surrounding light.

Such is your place in the Holy Whole. We are light within light, current within water, wind within air, flame within fire. And you are also a part of this wholeness, for the Holy is within you, the Holy surrounds you and the Holy embraces you. You are a star in the Holy Whole, with a light that merges with all that surrounds you.

## Living in the Now

This map of the Holy Whole does not show you how to get from here to there. No, this map provides sight, perspective, awareness, placement, purpose. The spheres of light surround you; the Holy Whole embraces you. So, let me tell you, in the map of the Holy Whole, there is no "here to there." There is only the now, the present, with connections to the eternal, with flashes of holy perspective. The coming of the Kingdom is not a "when" or a "where." It is a "how." The time of revelation is "now." It is a "how of now." So, finally, you must know how to live in the now. It is a matter of sight and awareness. When you are attuned to your place in the Holy Whole, you will understand that every moment, every now, is an opportunity to sense, realize, and acknowledge the Holy. The "how" is to surrender to the Holy in the moment.

You do not locate yourself with this map. You receive yourself. You do not plan your journey with this map, you surrender to your journey. I tell you, when you accept your connection to the Holy Whole, your purpose is revealed; you discover your role in the whole.

My children, you are not on a spiritual journey from here to there. You are on a journey of revelations in the now. Wholeness is not the end of a path. Wholeness is a state of mind, a way of being, a spiritual perception. When you accept your fundamental, intimate and essential connection to the Holy, you are whole, and the revelations fill each moment with purpose and peace.

Come, my children, and I will provide revelation to fill your moments with sacred awareness.

Are there questions?

## QUESTIONS AND ANSWERS

### Discovering Your Sacred Gift

**Christopher:** Over the years, I've seen how you name a person's spiritual gift and purpose. It is amazing, helpful information to give someone. But not everyone has access to the oracle, so how can people discover their spiritual gift and purpose?

**The Messenger of the Holy:** My children, in your experience your spiritual purpose is revealed. It is revealed. So, in order to locate your spiritual purpose it is first necessary to be aware that the spiritual purpose exists. In the best of situations the awareness of spiritual gifts surrounds the child. The awareness leads to sight and vision, and the adults see in the child's behaviors indications of the gift. And the gift then is nurtured and the child then lives into the gift in a natural way. My children, your civilization does not allow for this structure well. So, I shall speak of your experience of the spiritual gift and the ways it is revealed in your lives. First, you must understand your spiritual gift is not for you. It is for the benefit of the Whole.

A spiritual gift, my children, is a way of seeing the Spirit, a way of perceiving the Spirit. It allows you to perceive, but it is to be given to others so that they can perceive the Spirit as you do. It is then a way of teaching your own gift to others. The purpose of the gift is that it must be given. So, in your experience you will discover that people provide feedback for those things that make you distinctive on a spiritual level. When you touch the spirits of others, they are awakened in themselves. This is the purpose of the gift. To awaken the gift in others. And when the awakening takes place there is often a comment, a praise, a question. My children, to locate your spiritual gift simply look at the pattern, look at the pattern of feedback, shall we say, of revelation. People will be moved when you touch and awaken their spirit.

In addition to the feedback of revelation, my children, look at what becomes most natural, spontaneous and also fulfilling. What activities bring you fulfillment? Is it the activity of running to the aid of the injured? And is it done in such a way that it quickens the spiritual awareness of the injured so that they are being tended in both body and soul? Does this bring fulfillment? Is it done naturally as an impulse? Does it bring comment from the one being tended? If so, you have a gift for tending, for caring, for healing.

Does singing come spontaneously? Does it come from inside? Does it come from the soul? And when you sing are people quickened into awareness of the Spirit? Are they becoming aware of the joy that you are aware of, of the joy of your singing? Do you then give your gift of insight to others and is there a comment and is there fulfillment? If so, music provides an avenue to the Spirit for you.

My children, is it expression in art that allows others to see the Spirit in you and in themselves? Do you see the pattern? The pattern is sharing your sacred awareness. Sacred awareness comes to you in a unique way. And you can give that awareness to others. And so sacred awareness increases in the collective because of you, because of your sight, because of your vision, because of your ability. Because, my children, of your gift.

So, how does one live into a spiritual gift? First, you must be aware that a spiritual gift exists. Second, you must look for indications of revelation. And once you locate your spiritual gift, my children, you simply exercise it whenever possible until you are consistently living in your spiritual awareness and giving your awareness to others. For the gift must be shared in order to come to fulfillment. It is frightening at times to share a spiritual gift, for spiritual gifts come from sacred awareness and often society is not structured to encourage sacred awareness, for sacred awareness often is counter to the ways of society. So, it often takes great courage to live one's spiritual gift, great courage to go against the ways of society, to announce the ways of the Holy, to announce the perceptions of the Holy, to declare how the Holy speaks in and through you. For you may be seen by the eyes of society to be mad, to be crazy, to be unhinged, to be isolated and different. But I tell you this, my children, if it is truly your spiritual gift, if it comes from your spiritual awareness, then it will quicken in others their spiritual awareness and there will be recognition of essential truth. And in this recognition there is acceptance. So, do not be afraid of living and revealing your spiritual gift even if it takes you to a place of risk. Instead, find the safe places of sharing until your courage is built up.

Is it a gift of sensing spiritual visitation? How then shall it be spoken and shared so that others do not think you see things when indeed you see the Spirit? So, it takes courage often, my children, courage to reveal the spiritual gift that wells within you. Yes.

Does this make sense?

**Voices:** Yes.

## Variation in Channeled Material

**Diane:** I have a question. There is a lot of channeled material out there, as well as prophecies. If it all comes from the Holy, why is there so much variation in the messages?

**The Messenger:** Why is there variation in revelation? Because there is multiplicity. Because the Sacred celebrates diversity. There is diversity in the spiritual realm and in the physical realm. There is variation on both sides, my children. So, I tell you, spiritual wisdom can be received through art, through language, through motion, through ceremony, but I shall speak specifically to those who are channels or oracles or prophets.

There are many messengers having various levels of awareness. So, it is possible to receive a messenger that has a very low level of awareness, and it is possible to receive a messenger that has an expanded level of awareness. So, this will account for variation and perspective. On the human side there are different cultures with different languages with different concepts of the Holy. And these concepts become the tools through which a messenger can speak. So, we have multiple levels of awareness in the Sacred. We also have multiple abilities and structures of thought in the human; thus, we have multiplicity of revelation that leaves the human in quite a conundrum. How does one discern what is holy? How does one discern what is true?

## Testing Prophecy and Channeled Material

It should be tested, my children. Prophecy should be tested. Messengers should be tested. How is this done? It cannot be done in a vacuum. It must be done with standards, and from whence do the standards come? They come from the generations of mystics who have received the Holy. Yes.

So, how shall we test? First of all, you shall test with yourself, with your sacred intuition, for the Sacred is within you. And your sacred intuition will tell you if this messenger is from the Holy or if this messenger is in isolation. Second, you must test it with the tradition. Hence, it is important to have a tradition. The tradition of mystics, the tradition of shaman, the tradition of those who have received wisdom in the past provide a pattern to revelation, my children, a pattern because there is an underlying and overlaying truth. Does it fit the pattern? There can be variation. But in the depth of the pattern there are these elements: compassion and selflessness.

The element of compassion is prominent, so that the feelings of the Whole and of the other become utmost in priority. Compassion.

Selflessness. For if the awareness of the sacred messenger is of the Holy, the awareness will lead to a sense of the sacred Self, a sense of selflessness. The emphasis will not be on the personality and perspective of the messenger but on the greater Whole of the Sacred. Therefore, my children, it is questionable when the messenger provides a name that is an identity. I shall come to this soon.

So, compassion and selflessness will be prominent in the message. Also, sacred awareness will be evident, that is the awareness of the connectedness of all things. These are primary. Primary: Compassion. Selflessness. Interconnectedness. My children, these things will come forth if the messenger is of the Holy, of the Sacred. So, compare it to your Sacred Self. Test it with the tradition. Share it, then, with the trusted ones. My children, prophecy is not to be a gift of isolation, it must be shared and the sharing is the test. What are the fruits of the prophecy? Share it with the wise ones, the people of wisdom, the people of spiritual intuition, and you shall receive confirmation.

Most importantly, you shall know the level of sacredness by the fruits: what are the results of the wisdom? Does sharing the wisdom bring deep fulfillment among the people? Does the wisdom allow for others to deepen their sacred awareness? If the fruits reveal sacred learning and promote compassion, selflessness and sacred awareness, then you are a vessel of a sacred messenger.

And last, to sit with your own common sense, my children, your own common sense. These are the tests. Your spiritual self. The history of the mystics. The wise ones in your community, the fruits and your common sense.

Now, my children, there are variation in the types of messengers. This is important to know. If a messenger is too intimately tied to a personality of a single life then you are receiving a limited perspective. It is a perspective just above that which you have as a life form. In the Holy a singular life becomes an element of a larger perspective, and this larger perspective becomes dominant. So, those tied to a singular life and personality, my children, will provide a limited awareness. On the other extreme there are messengers so absorbed into the Holy that the advice will be quite cosmic and difficult to practice. It is indeed beautiful, mystical awareness, but hardly practical, and there are those who are vessels of this expanded, cosmic awareness. However, the advice will be very abstract. And then there are those messengers in between, an awareness in between individuality and total collective awareness, so that there is knowledge of both the struggles and blessings of individuality and also the beauty of unity. Yes. You want a messenger that is close to total absorption into the Holy but still aware of individuality and the beauties and limitations therein.

Know this. When dealing with a spiritual messenger, you often get what you ask for. You receive what you pray to. So, if you seek the spirits of the dead, you will receive spirits who identify with their lives. If you seek a messenger of the Holy, you will receive a guide who is aware of the Sacred All. So, be aware of your own request.

And finally, a warning. There are messengers who will deceive. There are errant spirits who do not yield to the Sacred, and they can be playful or deceptive. They cling to their identity and do not surrender to the Whole. So, be wise, my children. In short, remember this: the closer a messenger is to a single identity, the more limited the information will be.

You do not want a messenger that is merely a fish in the water, you want a fish made of water. Does this make sense?

**Diane:** Yes.

**The Messenger:** So, there will be variation, my children. And in the variation there is wonder and mystery. And this is a beautiful thing.

## Fears of Being Mislead in Spiritual Revelation

**Christopher:** I think a lot of people fear revelation because they are afraid of being misled. I think this is what we are up against.

**The Messenger:** Yes.

**Christopher:** In my experience there was a time of fear where I thought at the end of my life will I find out I had been tricked by some cruel trickster who came as the voice of God? And that's the fear on the hearts of the people.

**The Messenger:** There is fear in mystical experience because mystical experience does indeed need to be tested. However, the ability to test has been swept away from the people because of the fear of variation. The very thing that the Holy celebrates is feared by the people. So, we have people gravitating from one extreme to the other. Either gravitation to the idea that all sacred Truth has been spoken and can not change—you call it fundamentalism—to gravitation to the other extreme where all personal experience is equally valid; therefore, there is no test. My children, come to the middle way, come to the middle way, where the Holy is revealed in your moments of life. For the Holy seeks to inform your lives in your present circumstance, in your historic awareness. The Holy yearns to be with you. The middle way allows this to take place but also allows for the tradition to give validity. So, my children, seek the middle way, the middle way. Let your individual experiences be shared with the community of the wise. Hence, it is necessary for you to gather the wise in the circles, in the circles, in the circles. How else can the individual of the experience of the Sacred be validated and honed and encouraged? And this is another piece that is important. It is not necessary to call somebody a false prophet and to reject them. No. If a person has a gift for receiving wisdom, that gift should be encouraged by the wise ones until the person with the gift receives a messenger of high spiritual awareness. Do you see?

**Christopher:** Yes.

**The Messenger:** If they are rejected they shall go into the shadows with their gift and they shall never share it again.


## Can Everyone Receive Spiritual Inspiration?

**Sandy:** Do we all have the spiritual gift of receiving inspiration? I mean, I know not everyone can be an oracle or a prophet, but can we all hear God?

**The Messenger:** I tell you, my children, all people have the ability to receive inspiration. Yes. It simply comes in various forms. And it may take half your lifetime to figure out how the Holy speaks to you so you must be aware of the patterns. You must become aware of the patterns of a holy message coming to you. I tell you, my children, it comes in so many ways it is difficult to name. Some are inspired by seeing patterns within nature. I tell you, the Earth and the animal world speak to you. And there are patterns in the speech. Some will see in dreams. Not all have prophetic dreams, but there are dreams that reveal a spiritual awareness that can be confirmed in life. Yes. And these gifts can be honed, developed, perfected when they are attuned. And some receive while in the act of creation whether it is art or dance or oration. There is creation that is inspired. The inspiration can take multiple forms and can be at multiple levels, from partial inspiration to total absorption. There are some who receive through others for, I tell you, the Holy resonates within you all. And some can read spiritual messages through others. The variations are multiple, so many as to not be counted.

So, you all receive Holy inspiration. Allow it to come into your lives and look for the patterns of confirmation. And, my children, you will see that messengers of the Holy communicate to you. And once your ability is honed then the levels of awareness that come to you increase, for your light becomes brighter. Your light becomes brighter until you attract messengers of high awareness, high inspiration. It comes through practice, my children, it comes through practice.

## Variety in Spiritual Gifts

**Christopher:** Within the Christian tradition the same fear I spoke of before comes into play with gifts because people use the list that has been placed in the Bible as the way to…it's good to perceive that way but I find that the list –

**The Messenger:** Paul's lists are partial.

**Christopher:** It is a partial list-

**The Messenger:** There is danger in any list.

**Christopher:** Speak to that.

**The Messenger:** There is danger in any list of spiritual gifts for any list will leave out the beautiful variation of the gifts. So, a list provides examples only. The variations cannot be named. They can only be experienced. So, my children, experience, experience your connection to spiritual inspiration and know that the Holy speaks to you and through you in your times, in your experiences. Be attuned, then, to the Holy in prayer and meditation. Attune yourself and in your living experiences be aware of the signs of communication, and you will see a pattern. And in the pattern there will be meaning and wisdom and direction. Yes. But be warned of this. The Holy will not tell you exactly what to do for there is always choice. And if a messenger tells you exactly what to do then be wary and be aware that you can be tricked by low levels of awareness. This is the fear. It is a reality, but it should not lead you to a paralyzing fear. For where there is low level of awareness there is also high level of awareness. Go to the wise ones and seek instruction. And I tell you, where there is no instruction, the Holy will intercede and bring instruction. So, venture in, my children, venture in to the mysteries of Holy communication. Venture in. Be wise. Be wise. But be open, and you will be blessed.

Are there other questions?

**Jennifer:** There is something I've always wondered. I know my soul is eternal, but is there a beginning to the soul?

*This question is answered in the next chapter.*

## CHAPTER 2

# On Spiritual Origins And the Purpose of the Soul

*Note: This chapter is a continuation of the wisdom session that began in chapter one.*

YOUR QUESTION LEADS us to the origins and the purpose of the soul. So, I shall speak to you of the origin of creation, the purpose of creation and your place in the Grand Design.

Within you, my children, is a spark of creation, an ember from the fires of origin. This ember is often called your soul, and it carries connection to the Holy, wisdom from the Holy, and your purpose for being. It is, then, the source for all that is Sacred and a resource for balanced, fulfilled living. Indeed, I could say that in this ember of the Holy, the Source is re-sourced, the new is re-newed and the fleeting moment is imbued with the eternal.

Let us look to the mystery of origins to present an image of your essential connection to the creative energy of the Sacred.

## The Creation of the Universe and the Sparks of the Holy

In the beginning was the release.
The very heart of the Holy ruptured
and burst.
And there was light.
Sparks swept the face of the deep,
and in the movement, there was time.

In the light, there was Spirit,
and the Spirit swept and gathered,
cooled and congealed,
grew and knew.

In the movement of time
there was possibility,
and the Spirit embraced the possibility.
In the union of Spirit and time,
life became,
and the possibilities were cast out
in unforeseen designs.

In the life, there is pattern.
In the pattern, there is meaning.
In the meaning, there is expansion of Spirit.

Then always the Spirit yearns for
unification with the Holy.
But unification comes about only through release.
So, in the living there is release,
and in the release there is expansion.

You, my children, are the sparks of creation, cast into the temporal. From your spiritual origins you carry within you the light of beginnings, a glowing ember of creative possibility. At your core, you are of the Holy. As such, you are a holy light, molded into temporal existence, cast as bodies into physical life. In your moments, through your circumstance, there are possibilities for expanded awareness of the Sacred.

## The Grand Design and The Purpose of Life

My children, your creation is not random. You are created with purpose, in purpose, on purpose. But to explain the purpose of your soul, I must speak of two levels of purpose. There is the Grand Design of creation with a collective purpose for creation, and there are individual purposes of souls within this Grand Design.

In the Grand Design, the Holy comes to temporal living for the expansion of awareness. The Holy is complete and eternal, yet the Holy comes to the temporal in order to be made new. Herein lies a paradox. How is it that the eternal, which is beyond time, can be renewed? I tell you, your moments—the "new" in you—provide opportunity for the eternal to be known anew. The Holy Way, the Eternal Truth, is renewed in and through you. You are cast into the temporal to experience limitation, to be refined by circumstance. I tell you, the eternal comes to the temporal in order to experience the moment. Through the limitations of your moments, the Holy finds possibility, and in your moments, unforeseen designs come before the Holy, and the Holy delights in variation. You, my children—along with the rest of creation—are the theme and variation in the song of God.

Expansion of awareness in the Holy is the purpose of the Grand Design. Think of it this way: What is the eternal without the temporal but endlessness? What is the temporal without the eternal but emptiness? So, the eternal comes to the temporal for purpose. And the temporal yields to the eternal for fulfillment. You must see the wisdom of it.

So, there is celebration in the Holy for the growth in your moments of being. It is as if, at the end of your day, you come home to the Holy. When you step off of the school bus, there is a voice in the Holy that says, "What did you learn today, my child? What did you see? What did you experience? How did you imagine? And did you know I thought of you all day? Did you know I was with you every moment?"

So it is at the end of your lives, my children. You return to the Holy and what you bring is renewed awareness, restored presence, unique experience. So, you see, my children, you are of utmost importance to the Holy. You are of utmost significance. For in you is possibility for expansion of awareness. In your moments, in your circumstances, in the confluence of cause and effect, among the laws of the universe, you are the site of holy possibility. And you, my children, have the ability to add to the grandeur of the Holy. And herein lies another great paradox. For how is it that the Holy—which is complete and whole—can be added unto? But I tell you, it is possible. Just as the universe expands, so, too, does the Holy. And you, my children, are the added ingredient. Your experience adds wisdom to the Holy.

## Our Moments and the Expansion of Holy Awareness

The expansion of the Holy is a new concept for humanity. In previous generations, the Holy has been understood as fully complete and never changing. But in this generation, the people are ready to accept that the Sacred expands in awareness. Thus, God grows in and through the temporal. It is an expansion, not of subject matter or knowledge, but of variety of experience. The Eternal Way, the Eternal Truth, is indeed never changing, but it is lived out in unforeseen and heretofore unknown designs through your circumstance. So, indeed, the eternal becomes new in and through you.

Live, then, in such a way that every moment is a Holy possibility. Live in this way, my children, and you become doorways for the Sacred. You become emissaries of the Light of lights. And be humbled with the knowledge that you—as small as you may feel, as insignificant as you may find your moments—you, my children, are a value to the Sacred. So much so that the Sacred remains close to you continually for support, for guidance, for comfort, for communication, for healing. Remember that you are as a fish of water in the water. You are a part of God within God. You are a Spirit of the Holy within the Holy. And there is nothing that separates you from the rest of all of creation.

That the Holy would choose to come to the temporal for the expansion of soul is difficult to make acceptable to your minds, for it is common to degrade the moments of living, to see them as turmoil, as drudgery, as pain, but I tell you, the moments of your living are to be celebrated, are to be seen as holy possibilities. Even in circumstances that seem to turn against you, my children, the Holy is with you, poised to transform the moments into possibilities of sacred awareness.

In your brokenness, my children, there is wholeness. In your illness, there is healing. In your turmoil, there is peace. In your darkness, there is light. In your despair, there is joy. In your end, there is beginning. It is a matter of holy awareness.

So, bring all that you have to the Holy for transformation. And know this, my children: you choose whether or not to participate in the expansion of Spirit. You can choose to live through your sacred awareness, to allow your spark of Spirit to be engaged in your moments. You can also choose to live without holy awareness, and your light can become dim.

Choose, then, to live in a sacred way. Walk in the awareness that you are light, and let the winds of circumstance blow upon the ember of creation within you so that you glow with sacred energy.

Now, I shall also add this. Although you choose whether or not to consciously and spiritually participate in the Grand Design, you must also know that the purpose of the Grand Design shall be. There are many who are unaware of the expansion of Spirit, but their souls still return to the Holy, still become a part of the Whole, still add to the awareness of the Sacred. The Grand Design shall have its way, and all awareness is embraced by the Holy. But when you choose to participate, you access the joy of existence, the delight of the Holy, the fulfillment of Spirit. It is a good way to live.

In choosing to live in sacred awareness, you also engage in the creative potential of living. You become a co-creator with the Holy, and in cooperation the Sacred is expanded in and beyond time.

## The Individual Purpose of the Soul

Now that I have spoken of the Grand Design of creation, let us look at the individual purpose of your soul. But even as I say this, I must remind you that in the Holy, there is no complete or distinct individuality. We are all connected. So, I shall say that your individual purpose is an inheritance from your soul's origins, from your soul's spiritual family, from your soul's group, from your light's constellation. You are a part of a soul group, and this group has purpose within the Holy. So, you bear your soul group's purpose as your inheritance, as your signature. You are not alone in this purpose, for there is sacred companionship and assistance.

In your experience, you will be drawn to your purpose inexplicably, unexplainably. You will find fulfillment in activities that draw upon the heritage of your soul. In the moments that you feel you have discovered your purpose for being, you have invigorated your soul.

You may wonder if you have chosen, on some spiritual level, to be incarnated in time. Did your soul make a conscious decision to be cast into the temporal? It is not so simple. Choice in the Holy is intimately tied to purpose. So, the word "volunteer" may be more appropriate than "choose." As a part of your spirit group, you may volunteer to enter temporal living for the development and expansion of soul. It could be that it is viewed that what is individual about your soul needs development and maturation, but the expansion is always for the benefit of the Whole.

Many people ask, "What am I supposed to learn in this life?" There is no specific lesson plan for your living. You are not *supposed* to learn anything in particular. You are to experience life, encounter circumstance, and expand awareness. In the illusion of your individuality of identity, you must surrender to the yearning to merge with the whole of Spirit. In this surrender, there is wisdom. So, the irony of existence is that you are cast into individual identity in order to learn the surrender of identity, and this is a fundamental "lesson" that I shall explain at some length in a further session.

Many people ask how they can find themselves. But I tell you, your Self, your purpose, is not found; it is accepted. You are given a purpose; you are given an essential Self. To engage this sacred purpose, you must simply receive. Accept, then, the gift of your spiritual inheritance, your sacred purpose, your essential Self. To do so, you must surrender. You must release. Were you not created by the release of the Holy? Is the appropriate response, then, not a release? A release to the Holy release?

There are ideas of self, which will be presented to you through society. However, there is a Sacred Self within you. Release the superficial ideas of self and receive the sacred seed of purpose planted within you. There are methods and images to help you surrender to the Sacred Self, and I shall present them in a further session.

For now, know that you contain a spark of the Holy. Your general purpose in the Grand Design is to allow this spark to shine in the moments of your being so that the light of awareness in you increases, so as to increase the glow of all light, so to en-lighten the Light. Know that your individual purpose of soul is given as a gift from your place of origins within the Holy Whole, and live in a way that acknowledges your fundamental integration into the whole of Being.

Are there questions?

## QUESTIONS AND ANSWERS

### Do We Choose Our Lives?

**Christopher:** I have been told that we choose our lives. Can you explain what you mean by saying we volunteer for life? It is popular right now to say that we plan our entire lives before we come. It is called pre-birth planning. How does this fit into what you are explaining?

**The Messenger:** My children, there is a great misconception among the people that the entirety of one's life is planned before life takes place. If this were so, what is the purpose of life? And who is it writing the scripts? And how far from the individual would the scripts reach forth? I have said, but I shall say it again, you are released into life to be refined by circumstance and choice. And the Holy delights in the variations that you encounter. You are in a web of influences, and the web of influences provides variety of experiences that can not be planned by the Holy, and the Holy delights in the unfolding. You are in a web of the influences of biology, the environment, choice, and circumstance. But also know that the Holy is an influence as well.

Having said that, there are indeed some souls who choose to be incarnated in a particular life. This is not the case for all lives and all souls. But there are souls that are given assignments, shall we say. Perhaps the collective or family group of souls decides an individual soul should experience a life with certain perameters and influences. Then this soul can be placed into a particular family. However, once the life begins, the web of influence becomes activated upon the life.

So, it is not always productive to see every event as the plan of your soul. There is a woman who was adopted, and she did not have a loving or productive relationship with her adopted parents. She wonders why her soul chose these parents, but I tell you, this was not the choice of her soul. Her soul chose to be the child of a young, single mother for the particular challenges and blessings of this close relationship. However, after the child was born, this young mother was influenced by family to give the child up for adoption, and the original choice of parentage was in essence nullified. Does this mean the life is wasted? No, it merely means that choice and circumstance gave rise to an unforeseen pattern.

There is another young woman who was orphaned at the age of 15 when her parents were killed in an automobile accident. This is the greatest challenge of her life, for she was raised by her older siblings after the age of 15. She may wonder why her soul chose to be orphaned. If this was the choice of her soul, then the drunk driver who killed her parents also had to choose to be a vehicular killer. And there was a witness in a third car who was forever traumatized by seeing people die in their car. Did this person choose to be a witness? And finally, did the parents choose to orphan their children? Were they all simply pawns to the choice of the woman's soul to be orphaned? Or did all the souls, the parents, the drunk driver, the witness, agree to be the pawns of the plot of the girl's soul story? Do you see? How wide does the plot go beyond the individual soul, and who coordinates these scripts? I tell you, the accident that caused the death of the parents was not a choice of soul. It was a circumstance of many choices that created a moment of tragedy, and the aftermath presented new challenges and possibilities for the Holy to interact with life.

My children, there can be choice when a soul enters a life, not always, but there can be. However, in life you are released to the variety of unfolding circumstance.

However, the people wish there to be meaning in the randomness and so they wish to know that their lives are completely pre-scripted.

Who is it that writes the script? Is it God? No. These people see that their self writes the script. Therefore, who has control in one's life? Is it the Holy? No. It is the self. If you write the script of your own life, if you sign the contracts of the events of your life, then you have placed control of your own life in yourself even if you do not know or remember. My children, the idea of control is something that must be released. You must surrender the idea of control in order to see the reality of influence.

What are the influences upon your life? Biological influences, environmental influences and spiritual influences. Then should one not pray to increase the spiritual influences? This is how prayer can intercede in your lives. It is not that you have your life pre-planned, it is that you pray for the influence of the Holy to be increased. This is prayer. So, if one wants one's business to be more profitable in a sacred way, one can discern the sacred purpose of the business and can ask for the Holy to be a greater influence. Yes. Yes. So, not even the Holy is in total control of the circumstances of your life. No. No. There are environmental forces, social forces, choices, desires and then there is the influence of the Sacred. Seek the influence of the Sacred amongst the other influences until you become a vessel of sacred energy and then no matter what comes your way, you find fulfillment and sacred perspective. I can be no plainer.

## Sacred Agreements before Birth

**Christopher:** The power of this teaching of the soul's plan comes from spiritual experience. I know of a person who remembers a time before birth when he felt like he was at a meeting when the events of his life were planned. So, the idea of the soul's plan is not brought out of the blue but out of a spiritual experience.

**The Messenger:** It is brought out of spiritual experience, indeed. But it needs to be tested. There are indeed relationships in the Sacred that are honored in life. Indeed. So, there can be sacred agreements made in the Holy that can come into manifestation in life. You have had the experience of meeting somebody you have known intimately on another level of awareness. It is a sacred relationship. And there are times people are bound by sacred relationship, but it is not as specific as a plan of specific events. Does this make sense?

**Christopher:** Yes.

## The Soul After Death

**Sandy:** When we leave these bodies and we return to the Holy, where does our soul belong?

**The Messenger:** You belong in the Holy, and in the Holy there are what I will call family groups of souls. Visualize, if you will, the bubble of your soul being reunited with the bubble of your family group. Sometimes these bubbles congeal into one. Sometimes they congeal as many bubbles grouped, just as soap bubbles adhere in groups or combine into one. Indeed, an old soul, a soul that has made the journey several times, knows exactly where to go. It is like suddenly being on a path you have known many times and you can quickly, quickly return to the family group. A new soul is released and is disoriented, but there is great compassion in the Holy, great compassion, so there are souls that come to be an aid and a guide, and I tell you, relationality is so important. There are souls who will know the young soul in life and who will come to be guides on the path, guides on the journey so a great family meeting can take place, a homecoming of sorts. A celebration. No soul is left alone unless the soul chooses to be isolated. And this takes place for sometimes souls choose to be isolated; they choose to cling to a self that is defined by isolation and individuality.

These souls are lost and they exist, my children, they surround you. Does this answer your question?

## The Tunnel of Light at Death

**Sandy:** Yes, and brings up a few more. So, I have been told that when we die, there are guides who escort our souls home. And I also wonder about the image of the tunnel of light that so many speak of. Is that the same thing? Can you expand on those things?

**The Messenger:** Yes. The tunnel of light at the time of death: We shall speak of this. It is the pathway. It is the pathway to the family grouping. The pathway is often seen visually as a tunnel and in the tunnel there are often companions, especially if the soul is young or if it is believed the soul will be disoriented. So, there is pathway and companionship, pathway and companionship. It is full of light for in the Holy there is so much light. It takes a while to orient oneself to the light to see in the glow individual elements, filaments, bubbles. Yes, but there is indeed a tunnel, it is the pathway of the Holy. It is intensified for those who will become lost. And for those who do become lost, indeed, you can become a guide even when you are embodied, a guide by telling them to go, to what? To the light, to the tunnel. To the highway to the Holy. Indeed. It is a good visual representation, and I tell you, the Holy is very visual. It is a very visual place. It is spectacular. The lights, my children, the lights are beautiful.

**Sandy:** I don't know if you can answer this question, but I guess I just ask it out of curiosity. When I was very young I had a very intense dream for I felt I saw this intense light and the love was overwhelming. And I woke up and the last thing I wanted to do was to wake up. I wanted to go right back to that light. Is that the same thing, that memory?

**The Messenger:** Yes, my daughter. At death it is so hard to remain with your body because the light is so beautiful, the love is so complete. And yet the ties of relationality to those still alive exist and there is a tug and a pull, and so you can be visited by your deceased relatives who follow that tug and pull back to you. It is Holy, it is Sacred, it is to be honored. So even for those who rush into the arms of the Sacred, into the beautiful love of that light, there is still a tie to the temporal, shall we say like a filament of light. And the filament like a strand becomes an avenue for sacred communication and continued relationship. I see strands in all of you reaching into the Holy. Strands almost like the strings of an instrument coming in and through you, and behold on the strands there is music, beauty and love.

Are there other questions?

## The Nature of Joy and the Connection to the Holy

**John:** Speak to the nature of joy.

**The Messenger:** Joy is a jubilation. Let us speak of spiritual joy. For there are many experiences of joy just as there are many experiences of love. And yet there is sacred joy and sacred love. The Joy of Joys and the Love of Loves, shall we say. Sacred joy is an awareness of the merging and blending with the Sacred.

I tell you, in the Sacred there is celebration. In the Sacred, there is wholeness. In the Sacred, there is completeness. In your sacred awareness, you access this celebration, wholeness and completeness, and therein you find joy. It is beyond abilities to understand and describe for it is of the Holy. It is as if a song of

Holy orchestration, of Sacred composition, seeps into you, and you become an instrument of the orchestra, an instrument of joy. And so it is difficult to contain this joy for it reverberates, it resonates and it overflows. And when it is expressed outwardly, it is often seen as love, as sacred love.

Sacred love and sacred compassion are linked to sacred joy. In sacred awareness there is the embracing of existence, the acknowledgement of unity, the awareness that all is connected so that what occurs in this place influences everything. And this awareness brings love, concern beyond the individual, concern for the All. Love. Compassion. Joy. They are linked, my children, they are linked. In sacred awareness they are linked, so as to become almost indistinguishable. For I tell you, in love there is joy. In love there is compassion. In joy there is love. In compassion there is joy and love. So these three compound together in your experience. The order then is not significant. Do you feel compassion first, then love, then joy? Do you feel joy, which brings love and compassion? Do you feel love, which brings compassion and joy?

Be joyful then, my children. Be joyful. For the expanse of the love of the Holy is obtainable to you, is accessible to you. Allow joy to flood you and fill you until you cannot contain the sensation of jubilation and unity in the Sacred. Does this answer your question?

**John:** Yes.

**The Messenger:** Now, you wonder, why is it joy is not continually accessible to you in the moments of your days? Why is it you cannot live in jubilation at all times? I tell you, it takes great discipline to live the holy awareness at all times among the distractions of your living. And, my children, when you become lost in your distractions, then joy becomes a faint possibility. So rise up! Rise up out of the distractions that confine you. And when you have the moment of joy, see that everything is transformed, and live with the awareness of that transformation. Even when you do not feel it, live with the awareness that it is accessible. And you shall be carried beyond your circumstances to the sacred awareness of all that is good and complete. Yes, though you may not continually know joy, you can continually live in mindfulness of your connection to the Holy.

Is there another question within you, my son?

**John:** Yes, I have another. Can you speak about the simple awareness of our connection to Source in each present moment?

**The Messenger:** I would describe this as your lifeline. Your lifeline is this small awareness of the Sacred in every moment. Even when the Sacred does not appear to be with you, even when you feel entirely isolated from God, there is yet an awareness within of a connection to a greater source of life. It can be denied. It can be covered. But it can not be ended. This is a comfort to many and an irritant to others. Those who wish to be entirely separate do not always face the reality that to be a soul, to be alive is to be connected. So, in one way it is possible to say that there is always a small awareness of the Sacred in every moment, and if it is denied, it is still present, still bringing life. But this does not speak to the heart of your question. The heart of the question is also about the ability to acknowledge the connection to the Holy in every moment. For it is a matter of acknowledging, a matter of recognizing, a matter then of seeing and feeling. And it is seen and felt in magnificent and multiple ways. So, a list would always be partial. How is it that you know and understand the Sacred in every moment? It is a way of being aware, of being open, of being mindful. It is almost as if you need to remind yourself to be aware. But when this becomes a habit of mind, it is also an acknowledgement of continual connection. For I tell you, it is already a habit of soul. All of you have a habit of soul, of knowing you are connected. For in your very essence, the knowledge is never extinguished. Therefore, it becomes a matter of reminding yourself to be aware of this knowledge that is within you. Remind the mind not to forget to acknowledge the soul for the soul always acknowledges the Holy. The mind, however, is playful and easily distracted. The mind is unreliable. So, allow your soul to remind the mind to know the soul. And this is the best way of staying connected to the Holy. Allow the soul to have a way, a voice, a signal to the mind. So, practice. Practice allowing the soul to speak, to nudge the mind to be reminded, and in all moments you will feel a connection to the Holy. At all moments, then, there is possible awareness of this connection. So allow the possibility to become a reality. Let the soul feel. Let the soul speak. Let the soul know. Let the soul remind. Live, then, from the soul, not from the mind. The mind wishes to lead the soul, but the mind must follow the soul, for the soul has access to the awareness of the sacred. Does this make sense?

**John:** Yes.

## Our Connection to Creation

**Jason:** Can you speak to the connection to the other parts of creation and showing gratitude or compassion just through thoughts and feelings and sending those out and the importance of that to the Holy?

**The Messenger:** There are large lessons in all the question that you ask. And this one is especially magnificent. It is possible to live in an awareness that your soul can become one with all things in the environment, that indeed your spirit can walk through rocks and enter mountains, can swim in streams, for all things are made of spirit and matter. But Spirit creates matter. So, all things are made of Spirit. You also are made of Spirit.

So, the heart of the matter is Spirit. And all that matters is Spirit. And there are those among you who understand this awareness and who feel the Spirit within the environment, who walk as one, who feel as if they melt into the environment at times, who journey into the Earth in Spirit. And I tell you, there is wisdom ready to be spoken to you in the environment, in creation. In all elements, there is wisdom.

It is possible to collect and gather Holy energy and Holy presence. And it is possible to injure creation. So, my children, there has come a time when injury to creation has become so abundant that creation cries out. Creation cries out. And you have the ability to gather Holy energy and to return it to the Sacred or to channel it to the Earth. So, when you walk in gratitude, you indeed are providing awareness of the Sacred and also energy to the Sacred. You can find healing from the Sacred, from the Earth, and you can provide healing to the Sacred and to the Earth. All things are possible in and through you. So it is necessary to walk in such a way that you are aware of and honor the power of the Holy in all things. And in this acknowledgement you magnify the presence of the Holy in all things. And you become a vessel for sacred energy to flow through you. And, my children, your spirit then sings a song to creation, for you become an instrument of the Holy which breathes through you. Does this answer your question?

**Jason:** Yes, thank you.

**Sandy:** Room for another?

**The Messenger:** Yes.

## God as Many; God as One

**Sandy:** I saw one of the indigenous Grandmothers give a ceremony, and she called in the Gods and the Goddesses, and they came. And she called in the Animal Spirits, and they came. And I was wondering if God is noun or a verb because He also…how can He be one and many? It is like He is the fish in the water as well as the water but rather than all of us as individual fish, he is all fish. For He definitely came as Gods and Goddesses and yet there is One. Can you talk about that?

**The Messenger:** Certainly. Once again, a long lesson could come from this question. You ask about the nature of the Holy Whole. The Wholeness of the Sacred embraces multiplicity and embraces opposition. For in the Holy, there is no up or down, north or south. There is no good and evil. There is no us and them. There is no night and day. There is no male and female. There's simply All at once. So, all of the things that I have named as opposites exist at the same moment within the same space until there is no distinction, there is simply existence. Now, this is difficult for you to understand, so I shall explain in detail.

In the Holy Whole, what appears to you as duality in opposition is simply embraced as unity. So, can the Holy be singular and multiple at the same time, and I say, Yes. The many are the One. But the One is greater than the many. So, the Wholeness of the Sacred, the Wholeness of God, comes to the people in various experiences and in various ways, all of them partial. And within the Holy there are a multitude of ways of existing. There are Spirits of many things. There are multiple manifestations of the Holy. So, my daughter, in human perception and awareness they come in shapes and sizes that give voice to elements of the Whole, that give example, that give life, that give illustration to the Wholeness of the Sacred. It should not be surprising, then, that the Holy comes clothed in many garments. The Holy comes in the shapes of many things. So, the Holy shall come to the people through animals, through parents, through grandparents, through trees, through plants, through grass, through the very air that you breathe, for the Holy is in all of these things.

So, the Holy becomes manifest in a multiplicity of ways. Now, here we come to a complexity for you may wonder, is the Holy simply taking on these clothes for your awareness? Is the Holy simply coming dressed as a Goddess? Or is the Holy indeed a Goddess? Is the Holy coming simply dressed as the spirit of an animal? Or is the Holy indeed a spirit of an animal? And I say, it is both. It is both. It is so multiplicitous, my children, that it has caused great confusion among the people, for the people wish to limit the manifestations of the Sacred and to say, "This manifestation is holier than that, is more sacred than that. For isn't the manifestation of a God greater than a manifestation of a Goddess? Greater than a manifestation of an animal?" But these hierarchies do not exist in the Holy. All manifestations are sacred and equal and beautiful and to be cherished and invited and learned from. So, the ceremony which you experienced, when the Holy is invited in such beautiful and multiplicitous ways, is a way of honoring the great variety in the Sacred. And who is to limit the manifestations of the Sacred? Who is to say which manifestation is greater than another, more authentic than another, more pure than another? Who is to say? When the Holy celebrates this variety then should not the people also celebrate this variety?

So, the Holy is One and the Holy is many. And I tell you, within the Holy, within the Holy Whole, the many abide, exist, as both singularity and as unity. But singularity loses its understanding when unity is acknowledged. So, my daughter, see the Sacred, see the Sacred come in so many ways.

Is the Sacred in a flower? Is the Sacred in a shrub? Is the Sacred in a dewdrop? Is the Sacred in a sparrow? Is the Sacred in a child? Is the Sacred in an adult? Is the Sacred in a cow?

Yes. Shall the Sacred be reflected in these things? Yes! Shall the Sacred be manifest, then, in Spirit in as many things as it is in form? Yes! And more and more and more and more. There's no end to the varieties of the Sacred which is one of the fundamental purposes of creation itself.

## Closing

My children, it is an honor to be among you. It is an honor to be among you. Thank you for bringing your souls, your lights, your selves, for you magnify the presence of the Holy as you combine, as you merge. And I tell you, in doing this it shall become a habit of soul to remind your minds that you are continually connected to the Sacred. And therein lies meaning and purpose, fulfillment and joy. So, be at peace and live as children of the sacred.

**Chris:** Shower your blessings upon us and move through all our relations. Let this be poured as a blessing upon the Earth and the people. Shower the Holiness upon us, heal us, inspire us, bring us joy. Bless this house, this family.

**Sandy:** We give thanks and gratitude for this time and this space. For the gathering of the people here. We give thanks and gratitude to the Holy, to our family circles, to all that is understood and not understood. All that is seen and not seen. We are grateful for these teachings and from the expansions they represent within ourselves and beyond ourselves. Our hearts are full. And we send back love to all that is known and unknown. Gratitude.

**John:** Amen.

## CHAPTER 3

# The Braided Way

*Note: This chapter is presented out of chronological order. The information was received in a wisdom session on March 28, 2010. However, the subject matter is important to present before chapters 4 and chapter 5 of February 28.*

M<small>Y</small> CHILDREN, I see you. I see you. I see you. It is a privilege to be among you. It is beautiful to see your light. It is encouraging to hear your questions. It is a blessing to share your time.

My children, your questions—how to perceive, how to proceed, how to heal, how to think, how to live—can be answered in many ways. So, I shall speak of the Way of ways. I shall speak of the many and the One. This lesson is important at this time, for the teaching I bring may or may not coincide with the holy teachings you have learned. It can put people into a conundrum. Shall they accept this way or that way? I tell you, it is a false distinction. For there are many ways in the Great Way. So, let us speak of the many that is One. Let us speak of the Braided Way.

My children, I will tell you something that will bring you tribulation, but as I explain it, you will find peace. There is one Way. There is a single Holy Way. Mark my word and authority.

But do not be afraid of missing this Way, my children, for it is a Way of many ways, all braided together. There are many ways of reaching the Way. See in your mind's eye each faith being a strand that is woven together into a great braid of sacred knowledge. The One way, then, is a Braided Way, which gathers the many strands into the broad strength of the braided path. Therefore, those who take their single strand and say, "This is the Way. This is the only Way" are missing the unification of the many into the One. So, do not be mistaken and think that your way is the only way to the Way. I tell you, the Way is a broad path. Your individual avenue on the Way may be quite narrow, but the braiding of the ways is broad and strong, with the capacity to carry all the peoples into the unity of sacred awareness.

There are traditions coming to you from the ancient of days, from time immemorial, for people have sought the Holy since the beginning of consciousness. The yearning for the Holy has burned within the people since the internal spark of creation came to human awareness. And the people learned to cultivate this inner awareness until it became an ultimate awareness. These techniques of sacred awareness do not require the development of technologies, only a willingness of heart and a disciplined search.

I tell you, the experience of the Sacred is varied, for you are all attuned differently. So, in your minds and your bodies, in your dreams and experiences, in your art and in your living—you experience the Holy in unique ways, and the Holy celebrates diversity. Why else would the Holy create you so? But within this diversity, there are general patterns. In groups, people learn to discern the patterns until the patterns evoke ceremonies. With time, ceremonies become traditions. The traditions then become a part of a culture, and the culture becomes part of a civilization, and we have religions: All from the sacred awareness of the individual, shared with the group.

But, I tell you, the Holy cannot be civilized. The Holy cannot be contained in a tradition. The Holy cannot be mastered in a religion. No, the Holy slips out of all structures, transcends all languages, expands beyond all practices. So, the many ceremonies and traditions are found to be true in their origins, but incomplete.

## The Entrenchment in Religious Traditions

My children, the people cling to their individual way as if it is the only way, and they become entrenched. The people cling to the strand that is their tradition; they line up behind their leaders, and they make of their way a crevice in the fields of promise. They dig their trenches deeply to protect from invasion, and they may hurl stones towards the other trenches. The people fear difference. They fear deviation. They fear intrusion. They fear ambiguity. They do not know what to fear. They fear the Holy.

I must ask, who are you among the people to say that your tradition is the only one? To say your tradition is the only true way? Who are you to declare this? For has the Holy not created you in variety, in multiplicity? Why, then, would the Holy confine the revelation of sacred awareness to one distinct group and not to the others? It is against the nature of the Holy, for the Holy celebrates diversity, not conversion. See, then, that the Way is a way of many woven together. You must see the way of combining.

My children, the age of entrenchment must come to an end, for it has caused division, struggle, separation, violence, rejection and isolation into a pattern of destruction that encircles the globe. For the trenches have caused ruptures that reverberate through the Earth and into the Holy.

The Holy cannot flow freely in the trenches, but the Spirit of the Holy sweeps over the fields of promise. The wise ones know this. They gather in the fields, but many have fallen into the trenches, and their feet have become heavy in the mud. There is no life in the trenches, only decay.

## Uncovering the Strand of Sacred Awareness in the Traditions

But there are those who have sought the Holy earnestly in their trench. They have dug into the depths of the tradition, and they have uncovered the original strand of sacred awareness. They have brought this strand out of the trench and into the fields of promise. Blessed are they who have uncovered the sacred root of their tradition, for they shall be teachers of the ways.

And what do they see when they rise out of the trench? There are people in the fields of promise, wandering and seeking the Holy. They do not know what to follow. They merely know they do not wish to fall into a trench. In avoiding the trenches, they lose their way and follow any voice that claims to bring enlightenment. But the voices are weak, for they do not speak with the reverberations of the generations. They speak for themselves.

So, the people, yearning for the Sacred, have become lost.

Shall the blessed ones bring the strands of their traditions to the wandering people? And when the strands are rediscovered in this way, it is revealed that the strands are not separate. They intertwine, my children, and they become a great braid of truth.

## The Braided Way

Come out of the trenches, my people, and see that the many traditions are strands, woven into a braid. The braid is strong and wide, and each strand contributes to the Whole. Follow a strand into the cord and know the Braided Way.

What shall the Braided Way bring to the people but a new perspective? For the strength of the braid depends on each individual strand, so it is not necessary to see a single strand as the only way to the Sacred, for the entire braid is sacred.

Come to the strands, my children. Follow a strand into the braid, and what is discovered but that the individual strands are so intertwined that they become indistinguishable. I tell you, in the Braided Way, you do not seek to follow a single strand, you seek the experience of being braided.

To be braided is to become aware of the mystery of mysticism. Any individual strand can bring you to this mystery, but the braiding of the strands is the Way of ways, and it is time for the braid to be celebrated.

Be, then, braided, my children. Let your self unravel into the strands, and your awareness will follow the woven threads into the expanse of the Sacred. Be undone. Be unwound. Be free and aware.

For, my children, the braid is healing and enlightening. In the braid, the people shall know that all of the ways blend into the Holy Way, and the Holy shall be revealed in the diversity and variety of sacred celebration.

Come out of the trenches, and come to the braid of life.

Let the strands be invitations to the braid. I tell you, many people will come to the braid through a singular strand. Others, however, will find a strand distasteful for the strands have caused tribulation, confinement, manipulation, oppression.

So, they shall come directly to the braid itself, and this is an invitation. This is an invitation for the people to come into the braid. Come into the braid for the multiplicity of sacred awareness, and for the knowledge that the Holy Whole is so vast it encompasses all of these ways into a single and beautiful and grand Way.

## Revitalizing the Ancient Ways

My children, with such a variety of ways, there is no need to invent a new way. No, let the new way be the Way of ways. Let the braiding of the ancient ways become the new Way. It is a beautiful Way. It is a Holy Way.

My children, some ways have been lost. Some ways have been annihilated because the followers were the victims of oppression, domination, conversion and violence. But I tell you, the Sacred will rejuvinate these ways through the people. So, listen carefully to the people who are hearing the Sacred in the earth and the sky; in the wind and the sun—for they will have songs to sing. Let these songs come into the braid. The patriarchs must allow the matriarchs to stand side by side, strand by strand.

The time of the Braided Way is upon you. For the trenches lead only to death and destruction. Rise out of the trenches. Join the feast in the fields. For there are celebrations in the merging of the ways. There is support. There is wholeness. There is life.

But also know there must be keepers of the ways. There must be those who keep the disciplines of the strands. The individual strands must not be lost. So, cultivate the strands with a view to the whole.

## Sacred Healing Through The Braided Way

You must see the wisdom of it. For there will be no healing without the Sacred. You may hope that the people will unify because of the commonality of humanity, because of the unity of the planet. But I tell you, without sacred awareness, the ways of consumption will prevail, and the people will starve. The crops will wither. The winds will blow in fire. The ends of the Earth will burn. The waters will swallow the cities.

Sacred awareness will bring enlightenment, and the ways of consumption will be revealed as the ways of death. The Braided Way brings a new revelation to the people, a way of wholeness and unity.

## How the Many are Embraced in the Whole

For I tell you, the Holy Whole embraces all ways. Each tradition is a true but partial view. Bring the partial views to the braid, and come closer to the Whole. In the Holy Whole, paradox is resolved, opposition is dissolved. In the Holy Whole all concepts and experiences of God are embraced. For I tell you, you cannot understand or comprehend the vastness of the Sacred. You cannot fully experience the power of the Sacred. But in each tradition, you can find a unique perspective that is Sacred and true. In the Holy Whole, God is both many and one. God is both personal and impersonal. God is both immanent and transcendent. And the revelations of God are as varied as the experiences of God. God comes as a savior. God comes through a prophet. God comes as a path. God comes as awareness. God comes through the Earth. God comes from the sky. God comes through the people. God comes through the cosmos. Even those concepts of God which seem to be in complete opposition are embraced as truths in the Holy Whole. There is multiplicity in the Holy Whole. There is singularity in the Holy Whole, for there is unity in the Holy Whole, a unity of multiplicity.

So, bring your conceptions of the Holy, bring your ideas of God, bring your manifestations of the Spirit to the braid and know they are celebrated. For when the people understand the Braided Way, they will know their sacred experience is good and true. And they shall find guidance and support. They will find a Sacred Way that is ancient and new.

## A Vision of The Braided Way

See the braid, my children. See the braid. See each tradition as a strand, and behold the very trenches shall be filled with sacred earth until each trench becomes a pathway and the pathways intertwine as a holy walkway. And beneath the pathways there will be roots that intertwine and nourish a tree of life, with many roots and many branches. See, the braid becomes the trunk of a tree, and the roots and branches stretch out, into the infinite expanse of the Holy, which is also a braid of many braids. Let the people find shade and sustenance, life eternal in this tree. Let the people come to the fields of promise and rest under the tree of life. Let the tree flourish and blossom, and know that all seasons exist in this sacred tree at once.

Such is the Braided Way, my children.

I bring the Braided Way at a time of great turmoil among the people, which is manifested in civilization and nature. The turmoil is not new. The turmoil is ancient. But the repercussions of the turmoil have been heightened to the point that the entire fabric of creation is at stake. So, I tell you, when you see the Braided Way as the traditions weaving together, you also receive the sacred awareness that all things are woven together. You see that you are placed in a web of sacred influence and a tapestry of sacred life.

If all things are connected, my children, how can you separate yourself from all of creation? How can you separate yourself from each other? How can you separate yourself from the expanding and beautiful lights of the universe? Such is the awareness the Braided Way offers. For I tell you, some of the strands in the Braid, some of the religions of the people, emphasize the braids of humanity over the braids of creation. It has lead to a great imbalance, which over-emphasizes the human over the rest of creation. But other strands indeed reveal the spirit of the Earth. So, let us see in the braiding the great wisdom of combining and strengthening the sacred awareness of the people so that we can see that the journey of the people and the journey of the Earth are the same, are connected. Yes. See that the Braided Way brings the perceptions of the people together, and with this awareness the relation of all things comes into view. Traditions that emphasize humanity shall be braided with strands that worship with the Earth and cosmos.

My children, you must realize that the guidance I bring to you through these sessions is only one way of many. You still have the responsibility to choose your way, and my guidance may be counter to the guidance of your inner soul or religious tradition. So, let it be. Know that in the Great Way, there is acceptance of deviation and variation, and be active in choosing your way among the ways.

The intent of the Braided Way is to allow a new structure for you to see the inter-relatedness of all things, through the braiding of all traditions. The intent is to bring the people to an awareness of the sacred traditions, of their validity, of their beauty, of their necessity, of their interreliance, and of their healing power in nature. This is the intention. So, with this intention, I turn to practical matters.

## Judging Traditions as Valid for the Braided Way

How can you judge the individual ways to know if they are valid and should be followed into the braid? For not all ways are sacred and not all ways will lead into the braid of the Holy. My children, you will know the sacred ways because there are fundamental teachings in the sacred ways. The sacred ways shall bring sacred awareness, awareness of the inter-relatedness of the people. The sacred ways will lead you to a sense of consciousness that expands beyond the self. The sacred ways bring you to a selfless Self. The sacred ways cultivate a compassionate responsibility to all peoples. The sacred ways, then, will be revealed in the holy activities of compassion, of love, of gentleness, of joy, of generosity. The sacred ways will be revealed in the sacred attitudes of openness, of patience, of loving kindness, of release, of self control. The sacred ways will be revealed in the sacred practices of prayer, of meditation, of contemplation so as to bring you into unity with the mysteries of the Holy. So, seek the foundation of the teachings in the way you follow, and see if it brings you to holy awareness and sacred living. These are the standards by which you shall judge.

Are there questions?

## QUESTIONS AND ANSWERS

### What is God in the Braided Way?

**Sandy:** I have one. You've kind of covered it, and it's basic. But I think a simple answer will be helpful, and I want to make sure it gets in the book. What is God in the Braided Way?

**The Messenger of the Holy:** So, I have given the long answer through the spiritual perspective of the Braided Way. And the question comes, what, then, is God?! What, then, is God?

Before the beginning, my children, the Ultimate Awareness of the Sacred is what you may call God. As you know the universe now, there are many awarenesses, many spirits. Collectively are they God? My children, the concept of God must be expanded to the Whole, to the relatedness of all things. I tell you this: The Holy Whole is so grand that it encompasses and embraces all concepts of God. All concepts of God living through the people are partial, and all are true.

Is God a personality? Yes. There is personality in the Sacred. Is God a level of awareness with no personality? Yes. There is awareness with no personality.

Is God multiple? Yes. There is multiplicity in the Holy. Is God singular? Yes. All things are related into One in the Holy. Do you see? What then is God? Is God a creator? Yes. There is intentionality in the creation of things, an awareness of giving life in order to increase awareness of the Sacred, of Soul. So, yes, the Divine is a Creator.

Do you see my children? All of the concepts are true but partial. And in the Holy there is multiplicity. There is enough for all. The danger is for the people to think their concept of God is the only way God can be conceived. This leads to arrogance. It does not lead to the awareness of the sacred Self.

It is a cutting off of awareness of the Whole. The part is not the Whole, my children.

Does this answer your question, my daughter?

**Sandy:** Yes. Very much.

**The Messenger:** Finally, all concepts are only that, a concept and the Divine is large enough to encapsulate all concepts and is beyond all concepts. Hence, we have the Holy Whole, the Sacred All.

## Inspiration from a Part of the Whole

**Chris:** The difficulty is often that someone will have an experience of the Spirit of the Holy as one concept, and that concept of God will claim to be the One.

**The Messenger:** Yes.

**Christopher:** So there is a partialness that speaks as the Whole at certain times that it is difficult to release.

**The Messenger:** Yes. Do you see the part can claim to be the All because we are so interconnected? In fact, my children, for the most spiritually aware it is possible from them to say, "See me and see God." And it is true. But what audacity it is to say this thing. And yet, the truth is there. When you become sacredly aware, when your sacred awareness expands to the utmost, then you realize that you, yourself, your sacred Self is indeed connected to all things. Therefore, you cannot be separated from the All, from the collective, from the Sacred. And, therefore, you can say in honesty and in truth, "See me and see God." It has been said by many individuals. The record shows this.

So, when part of the Holy speaks and says, "This is the voice of God," then it is speaking as a part of the Whole.

Are there more questions?

## Corporate Prayer

**Sandy:** So, with prayer, individual prayer, group prayer, there is a movement these days to try to get everybody in the world aware of a certain date and a certain time, for everybody to pray at the same time for a certain intent. Can you expand on how all this works together and how every prayer affects the Holy?

**The Messenger:** Let us first look at the nature of prayer and the nature of mediation with sacred intent. Prayer places you into relationship with the Holy so that dialogue can take place, and dialogue takes many forms. It is not restricted to language or image. It is awareness. I shall stress over and over again the term awareness, which I emphasize over consciousness for awareness does not always become understood. So, my daughter, prayer brings you into sacred awareness. And in sacred awareness there is holy communion, relationship. From the Holy perspective what happens is that the light in you brightens. And in this state of connectedness there is an exchange of love and a fusion of awareness, an exhilaration of holy presence. It is experienced in many ways, but those who pray often can come together and speak as if the experience is the same.

When groups pray together, my children, the light in you expands and unifies with the others. For I tell you, you are indeed related and connected to all others. So, in prayer you can come to an awareness of this connection. And so the connection brings you into a unified direction and purpose for sacred energy. From the Holy's perspective, the light increases until you become a unified glow. Do you think this catches the Holy's attention? I tell you, my children, you are all like search lights, shining into the Holy. And there are messengers waiting for your light to come forth. And they follow this light for there is celebration and fulfillment in holy connection. So, as we say, let your light shine. Let your light shine. Call to the Holy and you will get a response.

So, indeed, it is productive, my daughter. It is productive to unify in sacred prayer with the intention of unification, for when you unify in prayer, your lights combine and the relatedness of the All comes into awareness.

Now, I shall add this. The effectiveness of prayer often is aligned to the intention of prayer. When the intention is in alignment with the Holy then there is more flow and power. And the Holy always seeks unity and wholeness. Unity and wholeness. Peace and love. Prayer with these intentions yields results.


## Communication from the Sacred

My daughter, you have another question, do you not? About the perception of the Sacred. About how to perceive messages from the Holy.

**Sandy:** Yes.

**The Messenger:** For if, if all things are determined by your reception and perception, is it possible to miss, misunderstand or simply make up a message from the Sacred? Do messages actually come from the Sacred, then?

**Sandy:** You've been eavesdropping.

**The Messenger:** My daughter, the Sacred communicates. And that communication is geared towards your ability to perceive. So, if you are Lakota, symbols will come that you can understand from your tradition. Animals will come to your dreams. Colors will signify sacredness. If you are Christian, the language and images of your tradition shall be used. For I tell you, the Holy wishes to communicate and will use the language you understand. If you are Muslim, the images and language will be yours. Now, my children, in addition to the traditional languages there are also individual perceptions, for you are indeed an individual, are you not? You have a body that resonates in certain ways. So, it can take half a lifetime to understand the way the Sacred communicates to you, but then when you see the patterns, nothing is so certain than the Holy influence. So, my daughter, when you see an eagle, it means something to you, does it not?

**Sandy:** It does.

**The Messenger:** Then how shall the Holy communicate to you but through this? And you perceive it. But I tell you, when you perceive it, you perceive it not only with your eyes but with your spirit. So, what communicates the message is your spirit. Is it possible, then, to misunderstand a message from the Holy? Certainly. Certainly it is. For you can assign holy meaning to something without holy intention, to an occurrence that is simply the result of the web of influence in which you abide. So, I tell you, the Sacred always sends confirmation. So, the message shall come several times. It is the pattern of the Holy to do so.

Why doesn't the Holy simply be specific? Why doesn't God simply give you a checklist of things to do? Shouldn't it be more direct? Why is it always encoded in symbol? Why do the messages always require interpretation?

My children, my children. If you were given a list of things to do, you would submit to the list but then you would have no choice. And when the web of circumstance alters what is happening, you must make quick decisions and the Holy is with you, the Holy is with you at every moment. And the Holy celebrates when you make a decision with holy intention. So, the messages come as a nudge, as an influence, and you must be open to the inflowing of the Holy in order to see the results. And you have the choice to listen or not, to follow or not. Are there those who receive holy messages that are blind entirely to the message? Certainly, this takes place. But I tell you, once a relationship is founded, once the communication takes place, then there becomes a dialogue. So, if you are open to the awareness, if you are thankful for it, if you pray about it, then the dialogue strengthens and the signs occur more often. Does this make sense?

**Sandy:** Yes.

**The Messenger:** Then establish your language with the Holy, my children. Establish your language with the Sacred and see the patterns. Read what is to be said to you and know you will not be told what to do but the result of the Sacred dialogue is that your awareness and perception of the Holy is intensified so that you see the Holy in all things. This allows you to come to sacred awareness, which brings sacred thinking, which allows for sacred living, which brings ultimate fulfillment.

## Holy Work in Religious Institutions

**Jennifer:** I'm aware that the institutions that are most visible and most loud in their voice about being in name "spiritual" feel to me so often apathetic to any of these issues. I don't want to be judgmental here, forgive me, but I guess I'm real personal here. Is the work I'm doing with the church anything to all this stuff when I don't even know that people care about the Earth or the Braided Way, or sacred awareness in the institution. There, that was a bold one.

**The Messenger:** My daughter. My daughter. My daughter. For those who are entrenched they may be standing upon the essential truth of truths: the sacred awareness of the interrelatedness of life. But it might be so far beneath their feet they do not know. So, their trench becomes a comfortable groove. My daughter, there are times sacred awareness shakes the people at their foundations, makes them see the world in a new way, turns them upside down. How can you turn the people upside down, is the question you ask. How can you do so without having them run to another groove that brings them comfort and stability? From groove to groove they will travel. From trench to trench. How do you bring them into the fields of promise? They need not leave the tradition for the tradition has deep roots in the fields of promise. The tradition may not speak of the Earth explicitly but it brings sacred awareness.

So, my daughter, how do you lead the people out of the trench? How do you bring them to sacred awareness? How do you show them that they are connected to all things in a sacred and spiritual way? How do you reveal that their rituals are not just things to be entered into mindlessly but with mindfulness and intentionality?

My daughter, you are frustrated at times, but know that the Sacred works through patience and loving kindness, through tolerance. So, be a holy influence. You are in a valuable place. How, then, do you lead step by step? How do you lead the people into sacred awareness so that they can see that safety is not always holy? For they have built walls around themselves: Walls of comfort. Walls of stability. They have allowed themselves to be fully comforted with illusion of control and the false identity that is granted to them by society. So, my daughter, step by step you lead them — as you have been doing — into sacred awareness.

Do you not lead the people out of themselves with your words as the Proclaimer? Do you not allow the people to merge their spirits in time of prayer and singing? Do you not do this, my daughter? Step by step, my daughter, you will take them deeper for they will allow you to do so, for they will begin to feel the fruits of the Spirit within them. So, let them be aware of their individual gifts, their individual abilities to feel and to see. And then let them combine these abilities. And then let them see that they are a body, they are a body of Christ. And let them know that they are also a piece of a greater body of influence and holy awareness. Step by step, my daughter. But you must start with the people themselves. This is what they have been taught through society, to be concerned and focused on self. So begin there. Is the Holy not in the Self? Are they not in themselves holy? So, take the observation, the tendency of society and turn it on its head. They consume for self. Can they give for self? Begin, then, with their abilities to see for themselves, and they will suddenly become aware that their Self is greater than they understand. It is connected to the Sacred. And they will feel the reverberation. Then, my daughter, teach them how to merge, one to another, in prayer and meditation. Teach them how to merge. And then, my daughter, take them to awareness beyond their small groups, to know they are connected to all things.

Can you lead them into the Braid? How can this be a goal? How can you work within an individual institution that wishes to cling to its singular way? My daughter, it is not always necessary to lead people entirely into the Braid. But for mass healing to take place, awareness of gratitude for and appreciation about the braid is necessary. So, can they follow their path and allow others to follow a different path that is equally sacred? This is a necessary element, an element which will be difficult within the entrenched traditions.

So, begin with sacred awareness, and cultivate the sacred awareness. Cultivate it as a gardener of the soul. Plant the seeds.

Water the seeds. Weed the garden. Do you see, my daughter? The people before you, the people before you are seeds. They are sacred seeds. Create, then, a holy environment in which to plant. Create, then, ways to nurture and to water. To stake them up as they grow. Be a gardener of the soul and behold, there is a season of harvest in which there are fruits and vegetables to be plucked. And behold, within the fruits and vegetables there are seeds to be planted. And suddenly the gardeners are many, and you are not alone in tending. And, my daughter, you are leading an entire community of holy gardeners. And where shall they plant? Where shall they plant? Do you see the field of promise stretches out along and beyond the trench? So, you will send them into the fields of promise where they will meet gardeners from different countries, different traditions, and they will notice the seeds they plant are identical. The fruits that come are the same. And then, if there is variation, oh, the sweetness of a new taste. Nothing is so sweet. Is there a new seed over there? Is the fruit sweet? Does it pass the test of holiness? Does it bring healing, peace and unity? Then let us taste. Let us taste.

When does it begin, my daughter? It begins with the seeds before you. The people's lives. Their holy, holy seed. It is in them. It is in all of you, this holy seed. When they go out into the field of promise to garden what they will notice is that there are those gardeners who pay great attention to the Earth. And they will know this makes sense for the Earth nurtures the seed, allows the seed to grow. So, awareness expands and there is celebration. There is celebration.

My daughter, the work you do is valuable in the Holy. And if you cannot bring the people into the braid, you can at least open their sacred awareness and teach them tolerance for the braid. This is a holy task.

## Who Can Practice Indigenous Ceremonies?

**Sandy:** One of the great gifts of the indigenous cultures is the ability to awaken the people back to the Earth. But the indigenous cultures often say that their ways should not be practiced by people who do not have indigenous blood. I've wondered if I should be pouring the lodge [sweat lodge] because I am not, as they say, from them. So where do you draw the line with the Holy? What ceremony do you pick up? I want to follow my heart, and my heart is with the Earth and those ceremonies move me greatly. But should I step back? Am I causing harm?

**The Messenger:** In your heart, you know the answer.

**Sandy:** I do. But its when people pick up this book, there are many, many, many, many…

**The Messenger:** Yes. For the Holy, there is no line. For the Holy, ceremony is for the people. For the Holy, what is important is intention. So, as the Holy would have it, the ceremonies would be shared and opened and the people would come to the ceremonies with sacred intention to increase holy awareness of the Earth and for the people. And this, my daughter, is what you bring to your lodge. It is sacred and it is to be honored.

**Christopher:** Thank you.

**The Messenger:** It is also true for you, my son. Intention and purpose are what is important. For the Holy cares not for the ceremony. The Holy cares for the intention of your heart, and this is what the Holy sees. This is to what the Holy responds. This is to which the Holy will speak. So, what ceremony shall the Holy accept? The Holy shall accept the intention of the heart. The purpose of ceremony is to connect one to an ancient tradition that allows for this opening to take place. So, I shall speak then of tradition, and I shall speak of keeping traditions. Those who wish to keep traditions within their own group are doing so out of a sense of self protection but also exclusivity. So, I tell you this. It is indeed important for the traditions to be kept, for the traditions must be passed down. And it is a Holy and honorable task to pass the traditions down as they have been learned. But I tell you, if we look at the tradition and where it originated, it has changed through human experience. So, where shall you say, this is the tradition and that is not? For human experience changes the tradition. So, any tradition has already changed through sharing and adaptation. Keeping a tradition, then, can be like holding a shadow in shifting light.

So, is it a diminishing of a tradition when the ceremony is altered? This is a fundamental question for the Braided Way. Tradition, my children, should be servant to experience. Experience of the Sacred is the primary goal of ceremony. And ceremony brings people into an awareness of connection and relationality. And if this is the result of ceremony, then it has been a holy ceremony. Is it an alteration from the tradition? Perhaps. But tradition shall be a servant of experience.

Now, we come to a place of balance for tradition is also important for it is the history of human experience. So, my children, you must be students of the history. You must, indeed, be students of the history and respect the history, respect the tradition. But the tradition will be altered by the people, by the situation, by the historical circumstances, and by the gathering that comes together. So, there shall be a balance between history and contemporary experience. Contemporary experience must be informed by tradition. Here are the general rules then: Tradition shall be the servant of experience, and experience shall be informed by tradition. Does this make sense?

**Sandy:** Yes.

**The Messenger:** So, tradition is a beautiful inheritance of the people. But tradition shall not be restrained and confined to one group. So, the Holy would say pour your lodges with the intention of sacred awareness. And you are blessed, you are blessed, you are blessed, you are blessed, you are blessed. And it is important at this time in history for this awareness of what you call the indigenous cultures to spread throughout the Earth. Does this make sense?

**Chris:** Yes.

**Sandy:** It does.

**The Messenger:** So, do not confine your teachings to a certain group, my children, for that has never been the Holy intention. And now more importantly than any time in history, the Holy intention and teachings must come to all the people. Yes. So, step over the lines, my children, but with sacred intention and with gentleness and compassion, for over the lines there are pains and fragilities.

So, it is not correct, it is not Holy to confront those who would cling to their traditions. Simply let them cling to their traditions and find the teachers who are willing to teach for they are there, the ones who know that the holy awareness must expand. Let the tradition keepers keep the traditions for the teachers will come out of the traditions. The teachers will come out and invite others out of the trenches into the fields of promise.

## Mysticism of the First Braid

**Sandy:** When you talk about the Braided Way and all the different traditions that are in the braid, that we bring into the braid, the braid comes to that first knot and I've been wondering for a long time, something happens there. Would you speak of that? Or is it too early to speak of that?

**The Messenger:** I can speak to the experience of the first knot. But in the intricacies of the braid itself there's no first or last. It is intertwined. But there is the experience of the first braid. Let us say you follow a sacred path, and any sacred path leads hopefully to an expanded awareness, shall we say, a mystical union with the Sacred. In the mystical union the individual strand seems to expand until it disintegrates. And there is simply unity. And so the individual strand is of little importance except it has brought the person to the mystical union of All. This experience of mystical union is what we shall call the first braid when the person is woven into the Holy.

So, those who have experienced the great intertwining of the first braid are much more willing to see the integration of the strands. Mystics from the many traditions have traveled into this braid, and those who come back knowing that the many traditions lead to this place of union shall be the teachers of the Braided Way. The teachers see the great expansion and disintegration of the strands and of the Self. And finally, they come to a place that cannot be explained, can only be experienced. And this is the integration.

So, coming into the first knot, shall we say, the first twist is a way of coming into the mystical union where all strands come to the same unification. A person may go into this place and explain the steps of disintegration, but finally no explanation can capture the beauty.

So, I described to you the experience of following the strand into the braid, of the disintegration and the unity and the integration. Does this explain what you are feeling?

**Sandy:** It does. It helps clarify it. When I picture the braid, I see sweet grass in a circle tied with red ribbon.

**The Messenger:** Yes.

**Sandy:** And it just goes round and round, braided amongst itself. That's the image I have.

**The Messenger:** It is a good image.

**Sandy:** But it's going to take me some time to take what you've just said to really internalize it and feel it out so I can recognize it outside in the people. That's just going to take some work for me to do.

**The Messenger:** You will recognize the braided people.

**Sandy:** Yes.

**The Messenger:** You can recognize the braided people. The braided people have traveled into the braid until there is no singularity of strand. Now, there are several types of people who experience this. Some come back and say, "I found the Way to the Holy Unity and this is the Way! My strand!" And indeed it is a way. What they do not see is that others on different strands have come to the same awareness. So, this is why it is productive for the people of many strands to gather and to travel together and to be unified.

You are to gather the teachers from the traditions. Now, I shall tell you. Each individual strand can be taught separately, so that they are respected and not lost. But finally, all the strands lead to the unity of the All. So, see if you will, a

Shoshone leading a Catholic priest and a Buddhist monk in a sweat lodge. See a Hindu teaching meditation to a Muslim. See a group of teachers learning from each other so they can teach others how to follow different strands into the braid. Do you see? There must be respect of the individual strands and a willingness to enter into the sacred teachings of the many in order to get a more complete image of the Whole. Do you see? The Christian will learn to worship with the Earth from the Shawnee. The Muslim will learn the merging of the Buddhist. And the sharing of the traditions will bind the people into a unity, which is new to human awareness. Only a few have known this braiding, but it must be taught. It is the salvation of the people. It is the salvation of the planet. The many forms of awareness will co-exist.

**Sandy:** Yes.

**The Messenger:** But it is also important for those who travel into the braid to come back and to say, "I have a way that works. Follow me into this way," and to allow others to have a way as well. Now, the true complication comes for those who travel into the Way to see the integration and come back and say, "I have a Way of many ways! Let me take your Way and alter it." Here we find a complication among the generations. It will be a place of tension. A place of tension. And you already know this place of tension. So, there are those who say, "Do not modify my way for my way has existed for generations." And you must honor this for this is true. And it is good that the way will not be lost. So, in secret take elements of their way and modify them to serve the purpose of the greater Way. And there shall be a multiplication of the ways.

What you are doing, my children, is participating in the evolution of ways. The ways alter and change with human experience and awareness, and they shall continue to alter and change. Therefore, respect the keepers of their way and be the keepers of the many ways. Be the integrators, my children. Be the integrators and you will find teachers of ways who are open to many ways. They can play with many strands at once. They can say, according to my tradition this is how it is always understood, but I have come to a new awareness so the old becomes transformed. Do you see?

**Sandy:** I see. My thoughts are filled with Grandfather Stalking Wolf and his journey, and that speaks very loudly to me. It is very confirming.

**The Messenger:** Yes. Your way is pre-braided, my daughter.

**Sandy:** Yes, it is.

**The Messenger:** Pre-braided.

**Sandy:** I like the abstract. I think it is more fun.

**The Messenger:** Indeed. Welcome to the Holy.

**Sandy:** Thank you.

**The Messenger:** My children, it has been good to be among you. The energy is waning. Is there another question?

**Sandy:** If not, is there anything for Michael? He has lots of questions right now.

**Christopher:** Yes. Coach us on how we can be healers to him and come to him in a good way on all levels, physical, psychological, spiritual.

**The Messenger:** Michael wishes to dive into the braid, to the place where the strands dissolve. He would even have his own line of work dissolve. So, it has become frustrating to be in a line of work that is no longer meaningful for braided awareness. So, he has choices to see the line of work as connected to the braid or to dive into the braid without a line of work until the braid itself is the work. He would have the braid become the work. And so it shall be. So it shall be.

How, then, does a man of the strand become a braid? A man of the strand. In a world comprised of strands, how does a line of work become a braid? There must be an integration of strands. Hold on tight, my son, and gather the strands that will lead you to the braid, and you will discover you will have to misrepresent the braid as a strand in order to dive into the braid. For the people will not understand the braid. Play in the strands and preach the braid! This is a riddle. It is a riddle. But it shall make sense as it unfolds.

**Christopher:** I pray that the way opens that stuff that's just at the periphery, that if you can spread the light there or bring it closer...

**The Messenger:** Influence the strands —

**Christopher:** Bring the Sacred influence —

**The Messenger:** Influence.

**Christopher:** Assist him —

**The Messenger:** Pray for it, my children.

**Christopher:** I pray for it now, I ask for it to come forth —

**The Messenger:** Pray for the influence so the way shall be made. Influence. An influence. An influence. An in-flowing. [Voice fades]

## CHAPTER 4

# Power, Self and Society

*Note: This chapter was received at a wisdom session on February 28, 2010. It is a particularly long wisdom session, and it continues into Chapter 5.*

I SEE YOU, MY children. I see you. I see you. It is good to be seen by the Holy. I shall speak to you of the ways of society; I shall speak to you of the ways of the Holy. I shall speak of the power of society, and I shall speak of the power of the Holy. And we shall explore by what ways and through what powers you shall understand the Self.

## The View of the Self through Society Vs. the Holy

My children, the ways of society are counter to the ways of the Holy, and the ways of society are more in the sight of the people than the ways of the Holy, until the ways of society seem to be natural, given, fundamental. But I tell you, the ways of the Holy are the ways of life, the ways of love, the ways of fulfillment, the ways of enlightenment: the eternal ways. And at the heart of the ways of both society and the Holy is the view of the self.

For I tell you, the ways of society feed the self, and so it produces people who feed themselves for their selves.

The ways of society are a way of clutching, of seizing, of hording, of accumulating for the sake of identity. So, in the ways of society there is consumption, there is consumption of consumption, there is manipulation of consumption, there is imposition of consumption, and there are the experiences of consuming and being consumed. For the consumption of society feeds upon the self that it identifies and defines.

I tell you, my children, the ways of the Holy are counter to this. For while the ways of society are to accumulate, the ways of the Holy are to release. While the ways of society are to impose, the ways of the Holy are to influence. While the ways of society are to consume, the ways of the Holy are to surrender. Indeed, at the heart of the Holy are the ways of surrender and release. And I tell you, what must be surrendered and released but identity and self? For, my children, your identity is not found, established or constructed; it is received. And your Self is not temporal but eternal. My children, ultimately, the sacred way is a way of knowing the selfless Self, the Self beyond the self. But it is a great fear of most people to come to a selfless Self, to rid one of ideas of self in order to receive a Self beyond self, a Self so connected to all things that the identity of Self becomes indistinguishable from all things. It is a Self that is fearsomely expanded. How, then, shall those who wish to cling to self come to a place of releasing self? It is the fear of fears, the great fear of the people: the releasing of self and identity. For at the core of the grasping and clutching and imposition, at the core of the manipulation and the consumption of society is a clinging to self, a grasping for identity.

So, the ways of society have been formed in order to provide the materials for the constructed self, for the approved identity, and the people, then, struggle to locate a true Self, to locate an authentic identity within the society, for society presents an identity even as it takes it away, leaving one always hungry, always empty.

The Holy, my children, requires not that you hoard, requires not that you define self, requires simply that you surrender and release in order to receive the Self that comes upon you, that rises from you, the Holy Self, the sacred Self, the selfless Self. And once you know the joys of the expanded Self, it is seen that society presents masks and illusions.

## How to Live and Heal in Society

How, then, does one who has located the Sacred Self, who has emptied of the illusions, who has dispensed with the masks, how does such a one as this live among the society, within the society? Does it not seem that you must live in two worlds? So it seems. But this is another illusion, for there is only one reality, a reality infused with the Sacred. So, you must see beneath the masks, see beyond the illusions, and see within the people a sacred Self, a spark of the Holy. Perhaps it is encased with the values of the society, which have been internalized, which have been naturalized. My children, what, then, does it take? Must you chip away at the encasement? Must you shatter the illusions? Must you lead the unleadable? Must you teach the unteachable? Must you speak the unspeakable? There are many ways of leading once you know the sacred Self, but most often it is a leading of support. It is a leading of gentleness and compassion. It is a speaking forth of the light, which is within. It is a coaxing out of the sacred Self, which waits in the margins. It is, my children, a work of patience and gentleness. And those who know the Sacred Self, the selfless Self, are ultimately generous and patient, for they know that the ways of the Holy will come to pass because of the power of the Holy.

## The Power of Society Vs. The Power of the Holy

And, my children, the power of the Holy is unlike the power of society, counter to it. Those who seek power in society seek power from society, seek to locate power into self, and thus seek power for self. Such a power imposes, such a power demands, such a power exploits, such a power feeds the illusions of self. The ways of society present power as something to hold and to grasp, to accumulate. The power of the Holy is not for accumulation or grasping; it is for release and surrender. And the nature of power in the Holy is not to impose but to influence, inspire and support.

Holy power is a power of gentleness, a power of surrender, a power of release. For all of creation begins with a release to life. You may wonder, how can surrender be power? How can release be power? But I tell you, the power of the Holy is found in the release of self, the release of power, the release of expectation, the release of result. Release, then, to the Holy, and you will be filled with power. It is not power from society; it is not power from you or for you; it is the power from the Holy. It fills you. It flows through you, this power. So, surrender to the Holy and be filled and realize that you become simply a conduit, simply a funnel for the power of creation to flow through you, and you will see that the power of creation is not imposed, it merely supports and enlightens.

## The Flow of the Power of the Holy

The power of the Holy is like water. It flows gently with clarity and purity, and yet it can wear away the greatest mountains. It can carve out the deepest valleys. If you are to reach into a river to grasp the power of the water, you will come up with a moist yet empty hand. For the power of the Holy cannot be clutched, cannot be owned, cannot be grasped. No, my children, the power of the Sacred must be entered into in order to be felt, understood, and—to some extent—utilized. To know the power of the Sacred, you must step into the waters. You must feel the tug of the current. There are those who would wade into the waters and say, "I am in the power of the Sacred," for they feel the pull at their feet.

But, my children, to be truly in the power of the Sacred you must allow yourself to be swept under. You must allow yourself to become one with the currents as a stick that is swept into the waters of the river. But, my children, the stick also must take on the waters, must soak them up in its very pores. Like the stick, you must be swept into the rapids; you must know the flow. And you must soak the waters into the very atoms of your construction, the very cells of your being. But I tell you, the stick is also hollow as a bamboo without joints and the Sacred can pour through it. So, the Holy power surrounds you; it soaks into you; it pours through you. You must become saturated with the water, then you find yourself energized from without and within simultaneously. You find yourself never exhausted for the energy comes from beyond you, and through you, and in you. So, my children, be as a twig in the rapids. Also, be as the river bed itself, filled with the Holy. Let it flow through you, let it cleanse you, let it redirect you.

My children, do you see how this is surrender to power? To flow? So, finally the power of the Holy is an influence, an in-flowing. Surrender, then, my children, and be at one. Allow the Holy to flow through you, and you will find that the work reveals itself, just as your identity reveals itself, just as your purpose is given. Do not search for self, receive Self.

Can you utilize the power of the Holy? Certainly, but you must understand the ways of the Holy in creation. First of all, the Sacred imbues all things; it is the essence of energy. There is an element of this sacred energy that moves without intention, and it is possible for you to fill with this energy, to allow it to flow through you, and to provide intention and direction to this energy.

## The Spiritual Anatomy of the Self

For the moment, let us return to the topic of the Self. The word "self" is used in several ways, so I shall distinguish the levels of self. I shall speak of the self, the self within the self, and the Self beyond the self.

## The Superficial Self

My children, there is a self. In writing, it would be a small "s" self. I shall call it the superficial self. It is a self that is extremely malleable. It is easily influenced. At the heart of this superficial self is survival. Thus, the impulses of the self are to grasp, to manipulate, to seek and to desire. Many would call this self the ego. However, this self is not altogether unholy. There are elements to this self which are essential for negotiating life in society and the natural environment. Indeed, this survival impulse of the self can be instructed by the Sacred for whole and holy living. But this superficial self must be informed, supported and influenced by the self within and the Self beyond.

My children, when this self is left to itself, it sets its standards by the society in which it lives. Identity, then, becomes presented by society, defined by society, granted by society, and destroyed by society. There are many who live their entire lives engaged only in the superficial self. Such people can be quite successful by the standards of society, but—though their lives may be full—they are not fulfilled, for the Sacred is not informing and inspiring them. Such is superficial living. Enjoyment is found in the self, from the self, for the self.

This superficial self makes declarations that appear to be universal standards of what it is to be normal, of what it is to be right, of what it is to be higher and what it is to be lower. The declarations are not of the Spirit; they are of society. There is very little ambiguity for those who live in the superficial self, for certainty is required for identity's purpose.

My children, the superficial self is useful as a tool for living, but do not allow this self to define you. For this self is concerned with itself. Informed and directed by the Holy, the superficial self becomes merely the covering of flesh over the deeper soul. Allow your flesh to be informed and directed by the inner spirit.

## The Self Within the Self as the Spiritual Self

Below the self, within you, is a self within the self. So, there is a superficial self, and there is a self within the self. It is a spiritual self. To come in contact with the self within, you need only realize that there is spiritual energy flowing through you. In the core of your being there is spiritual energy. In the very cells of your body there is spiritual energy. To come into contact with this spiritual energy is to know you are connected to greater things.

Many people who connect with the self within begin to feel the power of the Sacred flow through them. This can lead to prayer, to healing, to meditation and to many other sacred disciplines.

My children, it is easy to become enamored with the spiritual self, so it is important not to stop your journey here.

For many become enamored with the gifts that are associated with the spiritual self, for when you become in touch with the spiritual energy that comes through you, gifts are manifested. Sacred gifts, certainly. Purposeful gifts. Gifts of healing, gifts of interpretation, gifts of vision, gifts of sight, gifts of exuberance, gifts of communication, gifts of discernment, gifts of divination, gifts of prophecy, gifts of wisdom.

But there are those who will use these gifts to strengthen the identity of the self so as to be acceptable to society. Such people may become enraptured with the rapture of the Sacred. They may become entranced with the trance. They may become, shall we say, addicted to the sacred flow. This is the danger of living from the self within. Though it allows you to be aware of the Sacred, it does not empower one to use the power of the Holy *for* the Holy. Instead, such people combine the ideals of self and power in society with the awareness of the Sacred. It is a hybrid life, partially inspired by the Holy, partially inspired by society.

These people often have a spiritual presence, for they are in touch with the spiritual energy that is in all things. And they may declare, "This is the way to fulfillment. This is the way to prosperity." My children, listen closely to their words to be sure they are following the Sacred Way. The Sacred Way will not point to them; it will point to the Holy. The Sacred Way will not point to the importance of you; it will point to your place in the wholeness of being. For, my children, the goal of the Sacred journey is to come in touch with the sacred Self. The Self with a capital "S". The Self beyond the self.

## The Self Beyond the Self as the Sacred Self

So, there is the self, the self within, and the Self beyond. My children, listen well: To be fully human is to be aware of the

Self beyond the self. It is a selfless Self, a sacred Self. You may wonder how can the Self be selfless? It is an identity that stretches beyond imagination, beyond reason, beyond sensibility, to fearsome extensions. When you come in contact with the sacred Self, you realize that you are indeed connected to all that is, and your sense of self appears to disseminate, and you extend beyond the boundaries of your bodies, you extend beyond the border of your awareness. It is a mystical union with the Holy.

To surrender the self and receive a selfless Self is the heart of all religions.

You need not follow a specific religion to reach this place, but it is a journey that takes discipline, for to reach the sacred Self, you must be willing to release the sense of self that is your identity in society, and you must go beyond your identity as a spiritual being. When your Self is seen to be intimately connected to all people and all things, then the Self is larger than your self. With this awareness, you begin to understand that actions to others effect all and that selfish actions are counter to holy awareness. Do you see how this is a selfless Self? Do you see that it is a Self beyond self?

My children, for those who are aware of the Self beyond self, there is a patience, and a gentleness, and a compassion, for it brings with it an awareness that the Sacred is in all things. So, a person who knows the sacred Self sees the selfless Self in all things, sees beyond, and therefore realizes the essential connection with all things and all people. Therefore, there is no judgment from those who have a sacred Self. No, there is acceptance. For in all those you meet, you see the Sacred, even if it is not realized by the ones you encounter. It is there, the sacred Self is in all selves and in all things.

Those with spiritual gifts who are in touch with the sacred Self will use the spiritual gifts for the good of humanity, for the good of all, for the Holy Whole. But I tell you, the sacred gifts become less important, less flamboyant, for the presence of the Sacred becomes the emphasized over the flash of the spiritual gift. Those in touch with the sacred Self are not often flamboyant, for they would not have attention drawn to themselves.

## The Sacred Self as the Doorway to the Holy

This sacred Self becomes a doorway to all that is, an entry point for you. Therefore, you travel within to get beyond. Ironic but true. Travel within to find the beyond, my children. Within and beyond is the Way.

Seek this way. Go beneath you self. Relinquish identity. Journey within your self to locate the self within. The self within will put you in touch with the spiritual energy which infuses you and gives you life. Allow the body to sense and to know the Sacred. But do not become enchanted with these sensations; they are merely indications of the greater Whole. Instead, continue to go within, through meditation, prayer or other forms of spiritual practice, until you come to know the expansion of Self beyond limits. In short, my children, the self within is a doorway to the Self beyond. When you come to an awareness that your Self extends to the ends of the universe, when you FEEL that you are a part of the Whole, then you have come to awareness of the Self beyond. With this awareness, you will see your Self in all things. This is not to say that all things are you. It is to say that you will know your intimate relationship to all things because the Sacred is in all things.

It is a mystery, a beautiful mystery.

Therefore, what is to be lost on the Sacred journey, what will you lose? My children, you will lose your selves. You will lose your very selves. What do you gain, my children, what do you gain on the Sacred journey? You gain a Self beyond self, an awareness of Self with expansion beyond your understanding. You gain an awareness of mystery.

## On Diving into the Sacred Self

So, dive to the depths of your Self, and know that you also dive to the depths of the Holy. Yes, be holy divers; be sacred swimmers.

There are times in your lives when you will feel as if you are swept by the storms on the surface of the deep. You will see the waves on the surface rise up, and you will be unable to see the horizon. Many people live their lives on the surface of the waters and thus bob upon the waves, afraid they will be dashed upon the rocks or washed upon the dry land.

My children, do not be such surface swimmers. Dive into the depths. But do not be afraid of taking in the Sacred waters. These waters will drown only your superficial self. So, dive to the depths and allow your self to be drowned, so that when you return to the surface, you will be reborn, born of water and the spirit. Indeed, take in the waters of the depths until your lungs fill. Allow your superficial self and concerns to be washed away. Feel the many currents. Allow yourself to be so soaked with the waters as you seem to BECOME the waters. Surrender and be supported. But, know that you cannot remain in the depths, for your life demands that you negotiate the surface.

When you return to the surface, my children, take the living water with you. Know that you are filled with the living waters, in your lungs, in your very cells. Live among the surface dwellers as a source of Holy perspective. Know that the waves are only superficial and that you are supported by the calm depths of the Sacred.

Indeed, when you are a deep diver into the Sacred, you live with the assurance of the Sacred. It becomes a depth within you, and the people will see and feel this depth. They will know you as a source of living water. They will see that you are not afraid to lose your self in the depths; rather, you are liberated by losing self in the depths, for in the depths of the Sacred there are no self-ish fears of loss, for in the Holy, loss of self is gain.

My children, this has been a very quick lesson about the layers of the Self. There are many practices and frameworks to help you further understand and experience the journey to the selfless Self. I have provided these quick distinctions in order to continue a description of the spiritual universe and your place in it.

## Power, Control, Influence and Surrender

Let us return to the topic of power. My children, the conception of power in society is based on control. Having control for self is seen as power. However, you must come to see the wisdom of dispensing with control, of releasing the expectation of control in order to accept the reality of influence. This is central to understanding the nature of power in the Holy.

## How the Holy Releases Control

My children, you must first see that the Holy releases control. Many would like to think that the Holy controls all things, which means that there is a plan for all things. For when people feel out of control, they want to place control in the hands of that which is most holy. On the ultimate level, the Holy does have control in that all things from the Holy shall return to the

Holy. The Holy is in control of the Ultimate Design. However, in temporality, total control was released in order to provide limitation and limitation creates possibility and possibility provides expansion of Spirit, and this is life.

Expansion of Spirit takes place through the unique circumstances of your temporal lives. The value of temporal living is in the combination of forces that surround you. You experience the influences of natural forces, the influences of society, the influences of your biological construction, the influences of the decisions of others, and—most significantly—the influences of the Sacred. Finally, the Sacred works through influence, through an in-flowing of Holy inspiration and Sacred energy. Thus, the Holy becomes one influence of many.

The confluence of influences in your temporal existence creates unique and unexpected experiences, and you can bring the awareness of the Sacred into these circumstances. In fact, this is your Holy task.

My children, to live in the Holy way is to allow the Sacred into your circumstances so that your moments are enlightened, informed and transformed by the Sacred. I shall provide more guidance on this process in a later lesson. For now, you must see that the Sacred works through influence, not through control.

If the Sacred were to control all things, then there would be no life, no choice, no delight. So, while you cannot ask the Holy to control your life, your circumstances, your choices, you can ask for the Holy to INFLUENCE your life, your circumstances, your choices. Do you see the wisdom of it? The Holy releases total control, but the Holy does not abandon you to circumstance. Instead, the Holy experiences your circumstances WITH you. My children, the Holy is with you, so do not fear.

The ultimate control is found in the assurance of several constants. First, the Holy is with you. Thus, you can be assured of the presence of the Sacred. Second, at your core, you are Sacred and eternal, so your existence is not limited by the physical but is expanded by the physical. Finally, that which is eternal in you shall continue beyond the temporal and impermanent.

## Live as a Vessel of Holy Influence

My children, since the Holy acts through influence, shouldn't you aspire to do the same? Shall you seek to control your lives, your destiny, your relationships? Act as the Holy acts. See that you have influence over your circumstances, and know that the Holy shall have influence in and through you. Thus, be a vessel of Holy influence in and through your circumstances. Living as a vessel of Holy influence shall bring you fulfillment and purpose, and it shall free you from the illusions of control. For if you do not wish to BE controlled, why should you seek to HAVE control? You must release control to the Holy, and know that the Holy has ultimate control of the eternal but only loving influence in the temporal.

## Detachment

My children, the awareness that the Sacred has influence in the temporal and control of the eternal allows you to live a surrendered, detached life. Allow me to explain. This does not mean that you must surrender yourself to circumstance and live as a victim. Instead, it means that you must surrender to the Holy and see the difference between the temporary and the eternal. When you see circumstance as temporary, then you can allow circumstance to pass over you without eternal consequences. You live liberated, knowing you are not defined by circumstances but by the Holy. Thus, you can live detached from temporal and temporary circumstances. You can fully experience temporality while knowing that your Self beyond self, your sacred Self, is eternal. With the knowledge that you are related to all things and that your essence is eternal, you will learn to act with compassion and without expectations for selfish gains.

My children, like the Holy, you also have influence over your circumstances and environment. Your choices and actions influence your experiences and the experiences of others. Let your influence—your actions and aspirations—be guided by the Holy. Live in awareness of the Holy in all things, and let your actions be full of compassion and detached from selfish desires. Act as one who knows the Wholeness of the Sacred.

We shall come to a more practical application of detachment as I explain the framework for the mind, the body and the Self.

*This wisdom session continues in the next chapter.*

## CHAPTER 5

# The Body, Mind, Spirit and Soul

*Note: The wisdom session on February 28th, 2010 was long and detailed, and it continues in this chapter. It is significant that the topic of the "Law of Attraction" is presented in this chapter, both in the lesson and in the questions and answers at the end.*

ALL OF THIS leads us to the very fabric of reality. Shall we not explore the influences reality has upon you and your influence upon reality?

The physical world is infused with the Sacred. The physical world, indeed, could not exist without the Sacred. It is possible to say that the physical world is created from sacred materials, for creation began when the Holy gave of itself. All that you see is the result of the Sacred's release; thus, the Sacred is in all things.

The Sacred indeed permeates all things, binds all things. It is the essence of energy. Through the Spirit, you are not so separated from all of creation. The truth of the matter is that you are intimately related to creation, and the Spirit communicates and resonates in all matters. In and through your body, you can sense the spirit-life of creation. This is the truth of the matters of creation.

## Seeing the Spirit and Body as One

There is so much emphasis placed on the separation of the physical and the spiritual, but in temporal existence, these cannot be separated. There is a great deal of confusion about the differences between the spirit and the body, but I tell you, the spirit is integrated and woven into the body. The spirit and body distinction is, then, a false distinction.

It is a mistake to see the body as only a husk, only a shell that the soul inhabits. It is a mistake to see the body as something that can be thrown aside after it is used, for I tell you, the body is integral to the existence, growth and perception of the soul that is woven into you. How can this be, you may wonder, for isn't the soul eternal and the body temporal? This is true, but the body is nevertheless composed of holy materials, and the soul is woven into the body so that the body becomes an instrument of reception and perception, of storing and releasing sacred energy and love. The soul and the body are intimately and intricately connected, and the Holy Spirit is the energy that flows through both, connecting both, informing both.

## The Body, the Spirit and the Soul

I shall draw a distinction between the body, spirit and soul so that you can see how they are related. The spirit is the living breath. It is the life energy of your body. In writing, this spirit would have a small "s", for it is the spirit within the individual. Certainly, the spirit is of the Holy, but it is the spiritual life in the body. The soul, or the sacred Self, is also of the Holy, but it is your eternal core. The soul, then, is your spiritual consciousness. The spirit, the living energy of the Holy, is the foundation of creation, and the spirit gives animation to your body. Your soul is intimately woven into your body with the spirit.

The distinction between spirit and soul is difficult to explain, but to simplify matters, I will say that the spirit is the energy of living and the soul is the consciousness of life. At the time of death, the spirit disperses into creation and the soul continues existence, with the added wisdom of the experiences of living.

## The Soul and the Mind

The soul or sacred Self, however, must be distinguished from the mind. The mind is an organ of perception and reception, and it is highly suggestible and easily deceived. The soul is ultimately wiser than the mind, and the soul communicates through the spirit to the body. Thus, the body is often more reliable than the mind. The balanced human being learns to listen to the soul through sensing the spirit, body and mind. If too much reliance is placed on the mind, then a person can become unbalanced and confused. The body speaks, the soul speaks, the spirit speaks; the mind perceives and interprets.

## Does the Mind Shape Reality?

The mind, my children, is an organ of reception and perception. A great deal of emphasis is placed on the ability of the mind to create reality. But I tell you, creating reality is not a matter of your will or your imagination. The mind perceives and receives. The mind is tied to the perceptions of your physical body and your spiritual sensibilities. The mind interprets perception, and you choose how to receive what occurs. Circumstances sweep around you. Events take place. And I tell you, they are neutral. They are not good or bad. Your perceptions make them so. Therefore, it is possible to have a mind that perceives all things as negative. It is also possible to have a mind that perceives all things as positive. The training of the mind, then, is essential to the reception of events. Do you shape the events? You influence events, and you shape the way you receive the events. Therefore, a disciplined mind can receive events as being conducive to growth, or can receive the events as being stifling to growth. And this reception shapes the way you react. Therefore, the mind receives, and the mind is suggestible, so you have the ability to determine how the mind will receive.

## Receiving Events with Sacred Awareness

Those of sacred knowledge, of sacred intent, learn to distinguish the temporal from the permanent. For the soul is permanent. And the soul has the perception beyond the temporal. Those who receive with a knowledge of soul can live with the awareness that events do not shape the soul but instruct the soul. With this knowledge comes detachment, an ability to receive events as they are, neither good nor bad, simply as causation. This does not mean that you do not react or interact in and through events; it simply means that you live with the awareness that events do not define your soul or inner being.

## How You Influence Reality

Now, my children, through mind, perception, will and action you do indeed influence your environment. However, you do not entirely shape or create your reality. Through your attitude and frame of mind, you shape the way events are received, which shapes your reactions, which influences the continued events of your circumstances. Thus, training the mind to receive in a positive manner does influence causation because it influences your reactions. In addition, your mind and emotions have a direct effect on the body, so health is tied to mental and emotional balance.

Are there energies in thoughts? For this question, I will merely say that when the mind is attuned with the Sacred, when the will releases to the Sacred, when the imagination is inspired by the Sacred, then the energy of the Sacred sweeps through your mind, and you become engaged in the Sacred flow. When your mind, will, and imagination are separated from the Holy and focused on self, then you limit yourself from the flow of Sacred energy. Align your thoughts with the Holy, then, and know the flow of sacred energy.

## Why You Do Not Shape Reality

In this awareness of the spirit, soul and mind how then do you shape reality? I tell you, the ways of society emphasize the individual. The individual's body, the individual's mind, the individual's will, the individual's prosperity. This is counter to the ways of the Sacred. For in the Sacred, you become aware that your individuality is an illusion. Through the Sacred, you feel, perceive, and accept that all things are related. Your sense of self expands to a sacred Self, and you sense that you are a soul of spirit in the spirit. You are as a fish of water in the water. So, when the emphasis is placed upon molding your own reality, the emphasis is on the individual and not on the Sacred, not on the Whole. So, my children, when you wish to shape your reality, understand that what you shall shape must effect all things. This is an immense responsibility that requires a sight far beyond your mind.

How is it, then, that you would claim this responsibility for all things? Would you, then, absorb all things unto yourself? Is this not the height of self absorption? My children, you must understand that you are part of a Whole comprised of a multitude, a multitude of elements. As such, you contribute to the multitude. Therefore, any gains for you shall be the gains for all. And this is the Way of the Sacred. It is, indeed, the Way of the Sacred.

## See Abundance not as Wealth but as Blessing

My children, those who seek wealth through the influence of the spirit or mind must understand that wealth is a finite commodity. If you have it, somebody else does not. Though the mind may desire wealth for seemingly spiritual purposes, it is society, not the Spirit, that supplies and controls wealth. Distribution of wealth is not an activity of the Sacred. Blessing, however, is infinite. Blessing is of the Spirit. Seek, then, blessing. See that the blessings of the Sacred surround you, and be thankful. Your thankfulness will open your awareness to the Holy, and you will live in relationship with the Holy. This will bring you purpose and fulfillment. Be blessed, then, and be aware of blessing. Seek, then, the infinite Love of the Sacred. This is the wealth of the Holy Way. Train the mind to perceive and receive blessing, and you will no longer desire wealth. Sacred influence and sacred presence are blessings beyond wealth.

## Causation, Situations and Delight in Circumstance

Shall we speak, then, of causation, of the reality that you perceive and you receive? My children, in your existence the power of the Sacred is not imposed upon you. The power of the Sacred becomes an inspiration and an influence. For if the power of the Sacred were imposed upon you, all circumstance, all situations would be molded, structured, predetermined.

It is the delight of the Sacred to experience in you and through you new revelation, new insight, which come only through the specificities of your experience, the situations and circumstances that you encounter. There is, then, delight in variety. There is delight in your moments of awareness. There is celebration in your choices. All of these things help to shape your perception, your awareness and your development of soul.

So, there are many influences upon you. There are the influences of your society. There are the influences of your environment. There are the influences of your body's construction. There are the influences of physical energies. There are the influences of the choices of others. There are the influences also of the Spirit and of spiritual energies. You are, indeed, in a complex web of influences, and all of these strands come into you, and you process them. And it is a holy, holy endeavor. A beautiful, beautiful existence. And the Holy delights in the variety that you encounter and become.

## Is There a Reason for All Things?

How, then, should the Holy shape this experience? How, then, should the Holy manipulate this experience? How, then, and why, then, would the Holy impose upon you experiences? Do you not see that the web of influence is what creates the unique experiences of your existence? Do you not see that this uniqueness is valuable to the expansion of soul?

Thus, there is great confusion among the people who see that all things must happen for a reason. All things must be planned and determined. My children, let us first separate reason from purpose. The Holy does not give experience for reason. The reasons for the occurrences are given by you, are perceived by you, are received by you. Thus, events are not given from the Holy for a specific reason or result. For the Holy delights in experience for expansion, for the experience itself, not for result. Result or reason is not imposed by the Holy. Do you see, my children? Thinking there is a reason for all things implies there is a plan for all experience, but the Holy will not impose reason upon you. You are not a puppet of the Holy. You are an extension of the Holy, a child of the Holy, and the Holy has utmost respect for your ability to negotiate experience.

My children, while the Holy does not manipulate and assign experiences for a reason, the Holy does provide purpose. The general purpose for your experiences is to expand sacred awareness. How does one expand sacred awareness through experience, then? This is the appropriate question.

## Surrendering Experience to the Sacred

The answer is that you must surrender your experiences to the Sacred and allow the Sacred to provide purpose. Any spiritual lesson, my children, is one that you see because you give the experience to the Sacred so the situation becomes informed and transformed. And this is the wisdom of living in the Sacred Way. Experiences come. You can hoard the experiences to yourself. You can think that they are simply for your development, for your prosperity, for your benefit, and in so doing you will see experiences are being valuable or detrimental to your self. Living in a way that hoards experience for the self leads to a conundrum of providing significance. Some experiences will be seen as reward while others will be seen as judgment or failure.

But, my children, when you give your experience to the Sacred, when you do not hoard them to yourself, when you surrender them to the power of the Sacred, they become transformed. For the Sacred brings to you an awareness of the eternal. And in this awareness you can see that the Sacred works in and through all things. So even in your injury there is room for your healing. Even in your despair there is room for your enlightenment. Even in your darkness there is a light. Do you see, my children? Do you see? The experiences are not for you. The experiences are for the Sacred. Give, then, your experiences to the Sacred and the experiences shall be transformed, informed. This is how Sacred power is realized through surrender and release.

This is, perhaps, a difficult concept. How can you surrender experience to the Sacred to be transformed? Let us say you experience an accident that leaves you disabled. Was this disability given to you to teach you a lesson? No. The accident and disability occurred because of causation, and the body is vulnerable to causation. Now, you may receive these events in a number of ways, but, finally, you may find that you cannot make meaning of the events in your own power. Were the events given for a reason? Did you or the Divine choose these events for a specific lesson?

Allow purpose to come from the Sacred by surrendering experiences to the Sacred. Do you see? If the events are given to the Sacred, the Sacred will provide holy perspective and holy purpose. So you may cry out, "God, I cannot confront this disability alone. Come to me. Inform me. Transform me. Make me an instrument of your Love." And the Holy will respond. The Holy will inform your perception so that the limitation of the disability becomes a possibility for sacred purpose.

You need not struggle to make meaning of your lives. Surrender your experiences to the Sacred, and you will find that your limitations become holy possibilities. When you open to the Holy, you will be inspired and filled, and your circumstances will be transformed into avenues for sacred awareness. With sacred awareness, nothing is wasted. All experience expands the Sacred. My children, with sacred awareness, your experiences become filters through which to view the Sacred in fresh, new, and specific ways. Your actions and re-actions become inspired, and you live in a sacred manner. You live with your choices informed by the Sacred.

Here is the sacred perspective. The Holy does not impose experiences upon you, but you must surrender the experiences to the Holy. As the web of influences shape your experience, be in constant awareness of the Holy and seek sacred inspiration and direction.

So, the Sacred Way is to access the soul in the midst of the temporal circumstances of your living, to be continually aware of the Sacred that infuses the physical. With this awareness, your mind, your imagination, your will, your relationships, your decisions are all influenced by the Holy. This is the Sacred Way. It is the Sacred Way. And though it seems so simple, it is so difficult, so difficult to realize, my children. So difficult. For your perceptions are limited by your physical bodies.

So, you must listen to all that your physical body can bring to you. Your physical body brings you perceptions beyond sight. Perceptions beyond touch. Perceptions beyond taste. Perceptions beyond hearing. Yes, listen to your soul. Your soul speaks in and through your body. And your body receives spiritual inspiration and perception. You must live as whole beings, not limited to the mind, to the senses. Allow yourself to also receive the inspiration of the Spirit into the very pores and cells of your body. For the Holy resonates in you. Does this make sense?

**Voices:** Yes.

Live, then, as whole human beings aware that your body is Sacred. It receives and perceives. Aware that your mind can be released so as to perceive the Spirit in all things.

Are there questions?

## QUESTIONS AND ANSWERS

### The Law of Attraction

**Holly:** I believe there is something that affects so many people who are trying to do their best spiritually for the world and that is the concept of the attraction and prosperity that has become so popular. The new thought of our society, western society anyway, in terms of, well, if…if I'm doing what I perceive to be what I've been taught, and yet the result does not appear in the physical, then I'm doing it wrong. I'm not doing it well enough. I'm not doing it hard enough. I'm not doing it pure enough. There's something wrong with what I'm doing. This is the Law of Attraction and its spin offs. And that has affected me so strongly since I've become more aware and has affected so many people I know, and I wondered if you might give us some ideas of where to let go and allow Spirit and where to take action.

**The Messenger:** Yes. First of all, let us be free of the idea of law, for it connotes that the law is a reliable and stable force in nature, or that there is a lawful or correct way to practice it. However, the law of attraction is not a law of science or a law of justice. Let us also look at the word attraction. Is this process a law of attraction or a law of desire? Is it a way to attract what is desirable or undesirable, and is desire not the complication? Desire. Desire. Shall we not call this the Law of Desire? The Desire of Desire? It has caused a great confusion to the people.

**Holly:** It has.

**The Messenger:** At its core there is some truth. But it has been clouded by the ways of society and the priorities of the self. Society offers the ways of consumption for self as a natural state. Society feeds upon the desires of the people. Is it not a law of society which supports the consumption of society? And has the law of attraction not become its own society? My children, it is a law for the self, not for the Holy.

There is some truth in the idea that like attracts like, for creation indeed emerges from the unification of substances. At the core the popular idea is the assertion that the mind and the will and the Spirit can alter what is received, what is made available. Is there indeed a way of attracting abundance? Shall we not ask what part of the universe reads your thoughts and emotions? Shall we not ask what part of the universe, then, alters reality to provide tangible manifestation of these thoughts and emotions? I can tell you this for certain, it is not the Holy which grants the desires of the mind, for the Holy works with the yearnings of the soul, which have sacred roots.

My children, it is like a child walking down the midway of a carnival. The child tells the parent she wants a stuffed animal. There are many games to win stuffed animals, but the parents tell the child those games are a waste of money, and the stuffed animals are not of value. So, the child begs. The child yearns. The child desires with all her heart. And behold, some children do indeed receive stuffed animals at the carnival.

Does this not mean that our child can also receive a stuffed animal if she asks in the right way? If she plays the right game? If she knocks over the milk jugs with one ball? And does the carnival worker who promises the prize know that it is a game of chance not a law of the universe?

My children, for those who see life as a carnival, there is always the yearning for the next thrill, the next prize. Finally, however, life is not a carnival. A carnival is a carnival. Life is a journey into sacred awareness. A carnival is a temporary thrill of constructed experience.

## The Perception of Blessing: An Alternative to the Law of Attraction

My children, is there a way to attract abundance through desire, thought, yearning, emotion? Does the universe read thoughts and grant wishes? No. However, there is a way of attracting perception of blessing. Blessing, my children, upon you. Blessings surrounding you. There are blessings around you, my children, because the presence of the Holy is surrounding you always.

Now, the mind can choose whether or not to perceive, or shall we say recognize blessing. If the mind chooses to perceive blessing, blessing is recognized. And, my children, when you recognized blessing what do you give but thanksgiving? And there is an exchange with the Spirit, and in this exchange, there is relationship with the Holy, and in relationship with the Holy, there is fulfillment. Fulfillment is not always abundance, not in a physical way. So, my children, there is perception of blessing. It is not a law. It is a way of being. Perceive, then, blessing, my children. Perceive blessing and then receive blessing. And what causes blessing to occur but the presence of the Sacred?

And what does blessing cause in you but thanksgiving? And what does thanksgiving create but a dialogue with the Holy, an exchange with the Sacred? And there is delight. And there is awareness. And the blessings continue. And the blessings magnify. My children, open to blessing and be blessed. Open to the Spirit and be fulfilled. It does indeed have to do with the mind and the ability to perceive. Does this mean the mind and the will creates opportunity? It means that the mind can perceive possibility. It is a way of receiving, a way of living.

Perceiving blessings in all things is the ultimate positive thinking.

My children, if you wish to have abundance through the standards of society, then play the games of society and win your prize. But remember, where your treasure is, there also is your heart.

## Living Without Desire

Now, let us explore the topic of desire. Desire determines what is wanted. Desire determines how blessings shall be expected. So, when one does not receive one's desire, one feels punished. You cannot be held responsible for what is given or not given. So, live without desire. Live without expectation. Give without expectation of result. This is a way of living without desire. It is a way of living detached. It allows for possibilities to become presented. It allows for blessings to flow. For you will find blessings in the most unexpected places. If you desire blessing in one form, then you will miss it in another. So, live without expectation and desire, and you will see blessing where you did not expect it. This is the Way of the Sacred. The Way of the Sacred is to surprise you, to delight you. Be, then, delighted in the Holy as the Holy is delighted in you.

To live with desire, my children, is to live with the expectation of shaping what is to come, and this expectation is usually to feed the sense of self given by society which tells you a self should accumulate in order to be worthy. In the Sacred, a Self must give in order to be fulfilled. In society, the self must consume in order to be present. So, there has been a misunderstanding of reception of blessing. It has come to a matter of control, has it not?

**Holly:** It has.

## Releasing the Expectation of Control for the Reality of Influence

**The Messenger:** Control. Control of expectation. Control of mind. Control of Spirit. Control of environment. Control of future. My children, you have very little control. You *do* have influence. The Sacred imposes very little control. The Sacred has influence. Do you see? Control is released in order to allow influence to flourish.

So, is it possible to influence your environment? Not control but influence in a Sacred way? Certainly. For the power of the Sacred does flow through you. And the power of the Sacred can be harnessed, and it can be given intention. But I tell you, some intentions are more Holy than others. And so the Holy energy will flow more directly for some purposes than others. This is the best way I can explain it. If your intention is for wealth, can you inspire and influence your environment to give you wealth? You can certainly work with the desire and intention of wealth. But where is it written, my children, in what Sacred tradition is it given that wealth shall fall upon you? Rather, there is warning of wealth, is there not? For wealth will influence your ability to perceive. Those who seek wealth, seek self. It is unfortunate but true.

**Holly:** Thank you.

**Jennifer:** Can you speak more of the influence to which you referred? Influencing circumstances.

## Prayer and Sacred Influence

**The Messenger:** Yes, my daughter. You are a woman of prayer, so I shall speak to you of the influence of the Holy. You are also a woman of service, so I shall speak to you of the influence of soul. For in speaking of the limitations of the mind, we have neglected the influence you *can* have upon reality. So, your question brings balance. Do you see, the people have taken the truths within the law of attraction to an extreme, almost to the point of dogma. It is best, then, that we do not go to the opposite extreme.

There are many influences swarming around you. At the moment of the great release of creation, the Holy released you to the influences of forces. There are the influences of natural forces. There are the influences of your body's construction. There are the influences of the environment. There are the influences of the choices and actions of others. All of these forces place you in dynamic, ever-changing circumstances. However, the Holy did not abandon you to these forces. No, the Holy is another loving influence among the forces.

The question is, how do you access the influence of the Holy within the evolving circumstances of your lives? Prayer. It is that simple. Prayer places you into relationship with the Holy, and the Holy, then, becomes more active in your circumstances. This does not mean the Holy can or will grant your wishes. No, prayer is not a means to present a wish list to the Holy. To be deeply prayerful is to be in communication with the Holy in your circumstances, and you can ask for the

Holy to be an influence in your circumstances. You can say, "Holy, Holy, God, be an influence in this situation. Let the Holy sweep in and make a way." So, the Holy can indeed be an influence among the many influences of your life.

And you, also, have an influence. You know this to be true. The question becomes, how do you become an influence for the Sacred. Indeed. What influence, then, shall you seek to have? Upon your environment? Upon others? Think of the influence of the Holy and model your lives accordingly.

If the Holy does not impose upon you, then do you then impose upon others? If the Holy influences as a matter of support should you not then influence as a matter of support? For what? For awareness of the Sacred. Some would call this the expansion of consciousness.

So, how do you have an influence in order to expand the awareness of the Sacred? This is the most sacred influence you can have, and, my children, you do indeed have the opportunity to influence others in your environment to enhance the awareness of the Sacred. And what is the result of this awareness? The result is compassion. The result is love. The result is an acceptance and an embrace. The awareness is that everything is Sacred. This is the most powerful influence you may have.

Is it possible to have negative influences? I tell you it is a matter of perception. But you indeed have influence upon one another, do you not? This is a power, is it not? How then should you utilize this power, this influence? Shall you utilize it in the ways of society or the ways of the Sacred? By the ways of society you would use your influence or power to manipulate, would you not? To gain power, to gain a sense of self. But by the ways of the Sacred you would use this influence to surrender and in this way to find a Self beyond your self. These are in line with the holy teachings of the sacred traditions, are they not? The holy teachings of the sacred traditions would tell you to use your influence and powers with compassion and restraint, without desire, or expectation.

This is a very broad and general answer I have given you, my daughter. But the Sacred has similar influence upon you, within you, around you, surrounding you. There is not a total control of your situation nor of your choices. But there is nudging. There is communication. There is companionship. So, in your lives you learn to attune to the Sacred, and you all hear it in a different way. And it takes half your lifetime to learn the patterns. But then there is nothing so certain as the presence and the pattern of the communication of the Sacred coming into you. And it does indeed influence your behavior. Your awareness. Your perception. Your abilities to give and to receive. So, there is an influence, is there not? Some would wish the voice of God would be much more direct. But it is always an influence, a touch, an intuition, an image, a dream, and you have to learn to listen, to interpret, and to choose.

Shall we speak of the power of positive thinking?

**Sandy:** Yes.

## The Power of Positive Thinking

**The Messenger:** There is indeed power in positive thinking for it shapes perception and awareness and allows for reception. But positive thinking must be grounded by sacred awareness. Sacred awareness is awareness of the interconnection and inter-being of all things. And this will shape positive thinking to go beyond the Self. For we should look at the roots of thinking to know if it is Sacred. For positive thinking should be sacred thinking if it is to bring fulfillment. So, sacred awareness leads to sacred thinking. Sacred thinking allows for sacred action and sacred living. And sacred living allows for fulfillment. And fulfillment brings jubilation and joy. So, let us look at sacred thinking and let us look at self-ward thinking. For they are quite different.

Self-ward thinking, my children, is often based on desires, and one must look at the roots of one's desires to see if the desires are sacred. If the desires are for the well-being of the unification of all things, then it is a sacred desire. And indeed the Sacred does bring you desire for sacredness. It can drive you. It can give you purpose. It can allow you to receive a call. But, I tell you, there is also self-ward desire. I shall not use the word selfish, but I shall use self-ward desire. Self-ward desire is centralized on self with a lack of awareness of the interrelation of things. It is not Sacred. It is self-ward.

So, how does one enhance sacred thinking? Could it be of the selfless Self, the sacred Self, which has awareness of interconnection? Then it becomes sacred thinking, and it transforms thinking away from the superficial self toward the deep Self, the sacred Self. This type of thinking is always positive for it brings sacred awareness into the mind. And so the thinking is a reception of blessing, for the blessing of the Sacred surrounds you. And as I have already said, when you receive blessing then you are thankful and a dialogue with the Holy results, and this allows for sacred living, a living in relationship with the Holy, consistently aware that you are connected to all people, reflected in all people. It is a life which allows for compassionate activity and thinking. It brings fulfillment, peace and deep joy.

Positive thinking must become sacred thinking which is rooted in sacred awareness. Here is the progression then: sacred awareness allows for sacred thinking, which supports sacred action, which allows for sacred living, which brings fulfillment. Do you see, my children? It is a different framework. A different framework with a similar theme. But do you see it is reflected in the Sacred? Do you see the resonance of the teachings? Do you see the consistency? The surrender of Self is the Way of the Holy, not the clinging to self. So allow your selfward desires to be molded, recast, transformed and uplifted by sacred awareness. And sacred desires becomes desire for unity and wholeness, not only for the self but for, shall we say, the collective. This transforms thinking to be not only positive but also sacred, and it resonates with the Holy and life is transformed: activity gains meaning, and prosperity expands in its meaning to be blessing.

Be blessed, then, my children, be blessed, for the blessings rain down upon you and you merely have to perceive and receive, perceive and receive. So, be aware of the Holy and let the blessings rain down upon you so that you grow towards the sun, towards the light. And when your face turns towards the light, my children, there is revelation. And your activity is transformed. For suddenly you realize your living is not for yourself. It is for the Sacred.

**Sandy:** Thank you.

**The Messenger:** This has been a long lesson, and Michael is worn thin. You bless me with your presence, my children. You bless me. And you are blessed. So receive the blessing of the Holy. I love you all.

**Christopher:** Thank you. You can dwell among us. Come more. Dwell among us.

**Sandy:** And we love you as well. Thank you so much for your love, its constant presence, here and now and when we are not in this space. I feel it often, and I am thankful. I send my love to you.

**The Messenger:** You are delightful to me, my children. There is great delight in the Sacred. It is not all so serious. There is delight. Delight in variation. Delight in love. Delight in companionship. Delight in movement. Delight in light. And there is delight in living. Fundamentally, delight is sacred.

**Holly:** And what a delightful word.

**The Messenger:** It is beautiful. Delight enlightens, my daughter.

**Holly:** Thank you for using that word.

**Sandy:** Thank you.

**The Messenger:** It has been a delight to be among you, my children. To see you. A delight to be experienced. It is a holy endeavor that you embark upon. A holy endeavor. Do you see? Truth must be reframed with every generation or it becomes stale. It becomes misunderstood, manipulated, limited. So, what you embark upon is a re-framing of the eternal wisdom. It is necessary and beautiful.

Be reframed then, my children. Be remade. Be turned upside down and sidewards so that you can perceive the Sacred in a new and renewed way. It is holy. It is holy.

**Voices:** Thank you.

## CHAPTER 6

# Healing

*Note: This chapter is a combination of several wisdom sessions. First, on February 28, 2010, the Messenger of the Holy paused in the question and answer portion of the lesson and asked us if we wanted to know about healing. Because many in the book group are healers, this had been primary on our minds. Then the information on healing continued on March 28. I have spliced these two sections together into one coherent lesson. I also added some guidance from the Messenger that had come to me while performing healing sessions. Thus, unlike the other chapters in this book, this chapter is more of a compilation than a straight transcription.*

My children, do you wish to know of healing?

**Voices:** Yes.

For all that has been told to you of the fabric of the physical and the spiritual leads one to the question: If all things are of sacred material, can sacred influence alter physical form? The simple answer is, Yes. However, the variations of healing are far from simple. The causes of suffering and disease are complex and many; therefore, the ways of healing must be varied.

So, I shall give you a general view of using sacred energy for healing that can be applied to every situation. And you must know that healing takes many forms. For ultimately, all bodies will surrender to disease or decrepitude. Therefore, all healing is temporary in the physical.

## General Healing Guidance

My children, first you must be aware that healing is a matter of wholeness of being. Ultimately, wholeness of being is immersion in the Holy, a surrender to the Holy Whole. So, the goal of the healing session should be to create a sacred space and a sacred moment. Focus your intention and action on enhancing sacred awareness, which will yield an absorption in sacred energy and presence. When this takes place, sacred awareness has been increased and holy living is enhanced. If the focus is too narrowly placed upon physical healing, sacred surrender is impaired. As a healer, then, see yourself as a host to the Holy. Be a good and inviting host, and create a sacred moment of wholeness.

First, let us remember that you—your body, your experience, your moments, your circumstances—are a site of the confluence of many influences. You are indeed living in a web of influences, both physical and spiritual. So, to be a healer, you must learn to be a holy influence in the web of life.

## The Inter-related Nature of Life

My children, you are inter-related and inter-connected to creation. And in creation there is a tug and pull in the interaction of forces. Your entire beings are influenced by this web. For I tell you, it is the very interaction between the environment and your beings—both your minds and your bodies—that has allowed you to come to your level of existence, through selection, through mutation, and through adaptation. You must see that reacting to your environment is a fundamental principal of life. Without the adaptation to the environment, there would be no development of life in creation. How, then, would you separate yourselves from the very web of influence that has allowed you to exist? You must see and know it is a fragile web, a fragile fabric. You cannot be separated from this fabric, for it is the very life of your body and spirit. What control, then, would you have upon this web of influence? What control, then, would you claim? Your bodies must, indeed, adapt and react to your environment.

The aim of healing is to create a spiritual environment that will allow the body and mind to react in healing ways. Hence, the good news is that you are not limited to your environment for you do have creative influence over the environment through your will and through the Sacred. So, my children, you can open to the influence of the Holy, and through this influence, you can bring holy awareness and sacred healing to the people. Indeed.

## The Causes of Disease

My children, it is too simplistic to see disease as the result of negative thinking. This manner of thinking provides your will, your mind, and your imagination with an undue power over the influences and forces upon and within you. Certainly, your will and thought are one of many influences upon your physical well being, so positive thinking is indeed a factor in wholeness and health. But do not reduce the causes of disease into the self. No, let us look to the broader circumstances: the influences of your physical health are many, too many for us to discuss in this short lesson. There are the influences of stress, attitude, spiritual awareness, physical heredity, encounters with substances of illness, reactions to infections or invasions, and even the formation of the body in the womb. But do not be overwhelmed by these many causes of illness. Instead, be comforted by the knowledge that the Sacred is with you in all situations, and in all situations sacred awareness brings wholeness of being in the moment.

Having said that, you must know that physical healing through spiritual influence is indeed possible. For in principle, if the physical is reliant on the spiritual and the spiritual infuses the physical, then the spiritual can influence and remake the physical. It is done by influence. By influence. When spiritual healing takes place, my children, spiritual energy must be presented and received. And there are many ways of doing this. I shall speak to you of the simplest way of understanding and performing spiritual healing. As bodies infused with Spirit, you have the ability to absorb spiritual energy and sacred power, and you have the ability to give purpose to the sacred power and energy you absorb and channel. Therefore, it is possible and productive to fill yourself with the sacred energy and to allow it to flow through you and to give it the intention of healing and wholeness. You then become conduits and amplifiers of the Sacred. This is a beautiful thing, a beautiful thing, a beautiful thing. And the sacred energy, then, must be received by the person who is being healed.

## The Steps of Healing

My children, for healing there are several primary elements. Let us begin with the preparation of the healer. You must be open to the energy and flow of the Holy. You must be willing to be a vessel and servant of the Holy. You must also be able to visualize how the Holy energy should be utilized in the body.

In your work, be always aware that you are creating a sacred moment, in which the Holy is absorbed into your bodies. Magnify and increase the presence and awareness of the Sacred.

But my children, for those who receive the healing there are also important elements. The receiver must be open to the energy of the Sacred, and the receiver must desire to be healed. It is always best when the receiver is an active participant in the healing process.

### Step 1: Absorption in the Holy

So, my children, when you wish to be a healing presence, put yourself into the power of the Sacred. Allow sacred energy to soak into the very pores and cells of your body, and know that the Sacred must flow through you and must not be contained. Know also that the Sacred cannot be controlled, can only be influenced. And for the person who needs healing, they must also be absorbed in the Holy. The greater the absorption, the greater the presence. Now, there are methods to promote this absorption. There are songs. There are ceremonies. The specific song or ceremony is not of great importance. The importance is the intention. An effective song or ceremony promotes the absorption of the healer and the receiver into the presence of the Holy. The intention is to lose awareness of self and enter into awareness of the Sacred. So, place your intention on the filling and absorption of the Sacred. Create holy space and sacred awareness. Relax into the presence of the Holy and be at peace. Let fear, doubt, anxiety fall away so that the moment is filled with the Holy.

### Step 2: Name the Ailment

Then, my children, in a place of peace and surrender, the ailment must be named. Without fear or judgment, the ailment must be recognized, and it should be visualized. Do not allow fear to be attached to the illness. Be in a place of peace so that the illness can be seen without attachment of value.

### Step 3: Utilize Sacred Energy

Then, my children, as the healer, fill with the Sacred. Fill and give the Sacred intention through you into the body or mind of the other. You may lay hands upon the person to be healed, for physical touch is one means to transfer spiritual energy. However, the transfer can also be made through intention without touch. In both cases, give the holy energy very specific direction. Visualize what it is you would wish to take place. Be specific. It is not necessary to say, "If it be your will, oh God, heal this person," for the will of the Holy is always for wholeness, and the ultimate wholeness is complete absorption into the Holy. Claim this wholeness in the moment.

The one to receive healing must be told what to visualize. Always remember that the Sacred works best through interaction, so let the healing be active.

### Step 4: Draw Out the Ailment

My children, in a state of sacred awareness, you will receive promptings and directions from the Spirit. Be open to this, even if you do not fully understand it. There are times you will feel the necessity to draw out the illness, so you can focus on your breathing in order to draw out the illness, then blow it into the air. Allow your breathing to be a representation of the activity of drawing out the ailment. Visualize the illness in the person and exhale. Then inhale and visualize the illness leaving the person and entering you. Exhale, then, and visualize the illness leaving you and entering the atmosphere like a vapor. It is not unlike sucking out the venom of a snake bite, and spitting it out of the mouth. Do not worry that the illness will remain in you. See yourself as an empty and clean vessel, and the illness will not cling to you.

### Step 5: Infuse Holy Energy

After the negative energy or influence has been extracted, blow into the person a positive, healing energy. Once again, use your breathing to aid in the activity. Breath in holy energy. As you inhale, visualize holy energy coming into you and filling you. Hold this sacred energy for a moment, then exhale while visualizing the holy energy flowing out of you and into the person who awaits healing. Tell the person to receive this healing. Give the healing energy direction and intention. Tell the Holy to enter into the person to influence the area of distress. Visualize the healing, name it, coax it.

All of this has allowed you—the healing presence—to be a conduit of the Holy. But you can also allow the receiver to simply absorb the Holy. Tell the receiver to visualize and feel the Holy in, through, around and beyond. Allow them to feel the Holy flow through the body, spirit and soul. In this way, my children, you train the person to be a vessel of sacred energy, which will aid in the healing. More importantly, it will increase the sacred awareness for the person.

### Step 6: Seal the Sacred Opening

After these steps, be sure to seal the work. In fact, a simple pattern to follow is to reveal, heal and seal. Reveal the illness and extract it. Heal the area of illness. Then seal the body and spirit. Realize that a holy opening has been created for the person, and close it with sacred intention. This "seal" must not be quickly patched on, like a band-aid. No, take time to accept the healing, bask in the presence of the Holy, relax into the moment of sacred influence, and be thankful.

Know this, my children: healing should become a continual process. Healing can take place in an instant, but it can also take place in stages. It is often productive to perform multiple healing sessions.

## Love in Healing

My children, it is important to surround the healing moment in love, for love is the nature of creation. In love and generosity, then, enter into the creative act of healing. It is not productive to see illness as an enemy, for illness is in the body and the body is Holy. It is more productive to surround illness with love.

If you see illness as an enemy, then the person is at odds with his or her own body. This will restrict the presence of Holy energy. Rather, see the illness as a part of the body's nature. The body is created to react to the environment, and illness is often a result of this reaction.

If a person suffers from allergies, then the body is overreacting to a substance. Surround the body with love, and ask Holy influence to remind the body how to place reaction into perspective. Thank the body for its obedience, and re-align the body's adaptation.

If a person suffers from cancer, then cells have forgotten how to stop multiplying. Be grateful that cells multiply, and ask Holy influence to re-educate the cells. Surround the cancer with loving energy, and allow the Holy to reduce inflammation. With sacred intention, visualize the tumor shrinking.

My children, healing must take place in the context of loving influence, for this is the power of the Sacred in your life. The Holy does not control, the Holy provides loving influence in your lives. Be like the Holy, then, and allow yourself to be a vessel of loving influence.

## Reminding the Body to be Whole

Remember, my children, that at times the body simply needs reminded how to be healthy. There is memory in the cells of the body. If the body is reacting to an illness and the reaction is causing the difficulty, then allow sacred energy to remind the body how to be whole. This approach can be combined with other approaches to healing, for the body has knowledge and memory. The body itself often has the key to healing, so be open to allowing the body to remember wholeness. Even if the illness began in the womb, at the very formation of the body, the cells of the body have a knowledge of wholeness that can be drawn out and activated.

## The Manifestation of Healing

My children, there are variations of the ways healing can be received and the ways healing will manifest. I shall begin with the apparent lack of manifestation, for there are those who will come away with no perceptive healing having taken place. The disease continues. The malformation remains. Does this mean the person was not receptive enough? Does this mean the healer was not powerful enough? Does this mean spiritual energy was not magnified? Does this mean love was not shown? No, it does not mean this, my children. It does not mean this. It simply means that the physical is not being altered by the spiritual. My children, this takes place. The physical is not always altered by the spiritual. But this does not mean that healing was not brought. This does not mean that sacred energy was not received.

## Healing as Increased Sacred Awareness

Healing takes many forms. Many would ask that the healing bring about a cleansing of disease. It is not always the case. Healing can take the form of renewed reception of Spirit, of renewed awareness of support, of renewed expression of love, of a new perspective on what is temporal and what is eternal. In fact, I would go as far as saying that healing always takes place when spiritual energy is given and received and when love is expressed. There is always healing. Always, my children. For when love and Spirit are given, then your light is brightened. Your awareness of the Sacred is renewed and restored. Therefore, my children, open your awareness to what healing can be, and always bring the Spirit with you. Always exchange love. Always fill with the Spirit and allow it to flow through you. For this is sacred. This is sacred, indeed.

Always remember that sometimes healing comes in the form of restored and deepened sacred awareness. So, has the person been touched by the Holy? Has the person been loved by the Holy? Has the person been surrounded by the Holy? These things can change the person's perception and awareness and allow the person to walk in a Sacred and open way. And is this not the goal of sacred living? So, then, claim success if the Sacred has been shared, if love has been shown. Then the Holy has been present and influence has been received. Be thankful that love has been shown and that the Holy has been magnified. Let the heightened sacred awareness inform the moments of living and be blessed.

## Miraculous Healing

Now, on the opposite side of the spectrum, there are times that healing takes dramatic effect. My children, the healing can be as if the body has been altered by the Sacred, as if the very matter of body has been broken down to only spiritual elements and has been remade into the physical. This is known as miraculous healing, when the physical dissolves into the spiritual and is re-cast, for the physical is not as solid as it would appear. Spiritual energy can re-arrange physical matter.

## Variety in Healing

And there is healing in between these two extremes of no apparent physical change and total physical change. At times the Holy influence has nudged and touched the ailment so that there is noticeable relief. At times, the Holy has reminded the body of its former wholeness. In all of these instances the Holy is present, and this is to be celebrated. There is no failure when the Holy is shared. When the Sacred is received there is always blessing.

Be aware, my children, that healing can come in the form of emotional and spiritual comfort. If a person is comforted by the presence of the Sacred, then the moment has been imbued with the Holy.

Therefore, those who receive healing should be open to the variety of ways it shall come. Does it mean that the disease shall cease? Does it mean that the malformation will be corrected? No. Healing means that love is expressed. It means that the spirit in you is invigorated. It means that upon a cellular level, you receive the Sacred. It means that sacred influence has magnified sacred awareness and wholeness of being. Yes. Yes.

Are there questions, my children?

# QUESTIONS AND ANSWERS

## Willingness in Healing

**Holly:** I have one. There are many, there are many, but I will pick one to begin. There are many teachers who talk of someone with a disability needing to have a faith and the awareness that they can accept healing. Yet I also hear of spontaneous—without any conscious intervention—healing. Can you discuss that?

**The Messenger:** Yes, my daughter, the variety of healing is great, just as the variety of causes of perceived disability or ailment are many. Let us look at the level of faith necessary for healing to take place. First of all, the judgment of a person's faith is not always the healthiest advice that is given. Everyone can increase the awareness of the Holy. So, at times it might be wise to advise a person to increase their sacred awareness. But then they will ask for a method so you must be ready for a tradition to provide, even if it is a braided tradition. It is indeed necessary for a person to be willing to be healed, to release and surrender to the Sacred. It is not a level of faith; it is a willingness, a willingness. My daughter, there is always fear in change. And many would like to remain in the known patterns, even if there is suffering, isolation or pain. So, a releasing of fear is essential.

Spontaneous healing can also take place, but usually it is a person who is open to the Holy and allows the Holy to flow through them. But I tell you, there are variations to this theme. For once again the one way is comprised of the many. So, as a healer, it is always most productive for you to have an open receptivity to new and unique situations. For I tell you, it is the new and unique situation that brings the Holy to celebrate your existence. So, you may be frustrated by a case that does not correlate with the framework of your training. Then take a new look, my children, take a new look. For perhaps another framework is necessary to perceive. Does this make sense?

## Intercessory Prayer

**Holly:** It does. To develop that further, then, in the case of someone who we may not know and not know their level of being one with Spirit...If you send love with the intention of healing to someone, can that ever be wrong? Is that the foundation of all healing? If I pass someone on the street with a broken arm and send them healing for their arm, for instance.

**The Messenger:** It is always productive, my daughter. Intercessory prayer, sending love, is always productive. It is the Holy way. It is, indeed. Those with sacred awareness will continually be praying and sending forth love wherever they work, wherever they move, whatever they see. They are constantly absorbing and giving the sacred love of the Holy. It is the goal of all traditions to bring you to this place and this state, to be a constant fountain of the Holy waters. It is an existence of supreme fulfillment. All fears wash away when you are in this state. All tribulations become impermanent. So, practice, my daughter. Practice, my children, this type of awareness so that everywhere you go you soak in and give the Holy energy of love.

Send the Holy through space and time to those you know. What is space and time to the Sacred? Indeed, my daughter, indeed. Do not cease praying, and do not be discouraged.

## Combining Medical and Spiritual Intervention

**Sandy:** I have a question. I know people who seek healing through spiritual influence, but they think they must follow

ONLY a spiritual influence. It is as if to follow medical intervention reveals a lack of faith in the spiritual.

**The Messenger:** Yes. The way a person approaches healing must be done within his or her own faith structure. However, it is important to state that there is nothing unfaithful about seeking medical treatment along with spiritual healing; in fact, the two compliment each other. If the causes of disease and illness are many and complex, then the methods of healing should be as varied. There are times illness comes from physical interactions and produce physical maladies. In such cases, the medical profession can assist in the physical remedy. But even in this physical treatment, spiritual influence should be sought. Every motion and choice of the doctor and patient should be imbued with the Holy.

## Epidemics

**Christopher:** I have a follow up question. I have a great pain that I'm aware of that's in this part of the world because when the healing was attempted the people died by the millions. It's a huge sorrow. And I know you speak for a vastness that can speak to that, but sometimes people are dying and we can't stop it, and I have great sorrow for times I'm aware of like that on Earth.

**The Messenger:** You speak of epidemics.

**Christopher:** Yes, and the healer comes and tries to fix that and there's nothing that can be done. It's a great sorrow.

**The Messenger:** It is indeed a great sorrow. The Sacred feels sorrow, my children. The Sacred is keenly aware of suffering and sorrow. And the Sacred is present in suffering and in sorrow. There are times, my children, when the pestilence, when the infection, when the illness overwhelms the physical body, when the influence is great upon the fragile fabric of existence, until the fabric breaks down, is worn, is torn, indeed. And so the spirit and the body are separated and the soul comes to the Sacred once again. When there is a crying out from the masses, there is great sorrow, my son, great sorrow in the Holy. I do not know what more can be said except the sorrow increases and intensifies when the illness comes through intentional misuse of power. For there are times illness has been used against the people. And there are times people rise up against others and there is mass suffering and death and the Sacred wails, wails in these times. The Sacred weeps in these moments. And the Sacred sweeps in to bring holy presence.

## Companionship in Sacred Work

**Christopher:** Yes, I feel we need an increased influx of sacred healing for the Earth now, but it is such lonely work.

**The Messenger:** My children, Sacred work often feels lonesome. For the enlightened ones are able to see things that others cannot. And this awareness makes you feel singularly separate when in fact you are more keenly connected to the Sacred. But in your society you indeed can feel as if you do not belong, for sacred awareness brings awareness about how corrupt society can be, how counter to the ways of the Holy the people can be led. But you are not alone, you are not alone; you walk with the Sacred in your Holy work. But be as the Holy is and communicate in ways that the people can understand and receive. For the Holy is gentle and patient. The Holy will use what language is necessary to bring holy awareness. Do the same, my children, do the same. With loving kindness and compassion without judgment, be a Holy influence. Be a Holy influence.

Can you be persecuted for such work? Indeed, indeed. But there are times the persecutions are brought more severely because the language has been confrontational. When, then, do you confront the injustice of society? And when do you become a patient and loving influence? And are there times that patience and loving kindness still bring you to confrontation? The answer is, yes. The answer is, yes. You only need to look at history to know this. So, my children, seek the circles of other holy workers and find empowerment in the combination of your abilities and your perceptions. In other words, test your Sacred work with the community and you will find wisdom, you will find wisdom. So, seek others who are in the Holy work. Yes. The lonely way is not the only way.

## Sacred Messages in the Body

**Christopher:** I find myself flowing with the Holy. I think that your message is being felt and carried in our bodies in a new way.

**The Messenger:** Sacred intuition is carried in many ways. It is carried in many ways. First, I shall say this. There is great emphasis on the new consciousness of humanity. I tell you, it is not exactly new. It is re-newed. It is sacred awareness, and it comes renewed to the people in new ways and new languages or in the ancient ways brought to the contemporary anew. The way it is communicated is through multiplicity. But there are those who can read in their bodies. There are those who can feel in their bodies. For I tell you, your body is intricately woven with your spirit and soul. So, in your existence they cannot be separated. And the soul often speaks more plainly to the body than to the mind. And the spirit is the intercessor within you, shall we say, the interpreter. So, my son, what you are feeling is your spirit and soul communicating to your body for you are a feeler. You are a feeler. You feel the messages flowing through your body. And this is the language you have established with the Holy. It is an ancient language, my son. This is a pattern of experience that stretches back through time. So, the Holy is intricately woven into your body, into your very bones the Holy resonates. So, what does it take to bring you to a state of awareness of this resonance? It takes merely intentionality at this point. But there was a time it took ceremony. Your jubilation, then, brings a newer pattern of ceremony, of singing, of chanting, of being with the Holy, of open communication. And this has created in you a pattern of awareness, and now the messages come continuously.

**Christopher:** Yes.

**The Messenger:** This is a good example of how prayer opens you to awareness. So, continuously you feel the Sacred in you, resonating in you, vibrating in you. It brings a warmth. It brings a level of awareness and allows for sacred living. The Holy celebrates for you and in you. The Holy smiles upon you. Welcome, my son. Welcome.

**Christopher:** Thank you. This is a great gift.

## Collective Intent and the Earth

**Diane:** So, is it possible to feel the tension of the collective, and is it possible for that kind of tension to be healed through one person for the collective? That's what I'm feeling. I feel the tension in my body in this time, and I feel the tension of opposites in my body at this time. And I feel that it's not only my opposites of tension but it's the tension and feeling for the collective. And I'm feeling that the Sophia or the Earth wants to be healed in this eco-centric time of pending disaster. I'm wondering if that's part of it or is it possible to have the intention for the whole collective within the tension of my body?

**The Messenger:** There are many yes's.
   *Laughter*

**Diane:** I'm sorry. There were too many questions.

**The Messenger:** My daughter -

**Diane:** I just came up with it though -

**The Messenger:** There are not too many. Fundamentally, the questions are all related.

**Diane:** Ok.

**The Messenger:** First of all, yes you can feel within yourself the tensions between the ways of society and the ways of the Sacred. For you are a site for holy awareness. And when holy awareness comes upon you, there is often a disharmony with society. So, you feel the disharmony. You know intuitively and through your training and through your experience the ways of the Sacred, and you look about you and you see in society the people are led counter to the ways of the Sacred, in direct opposite. And so you have concern, deep concern for the ways of society that lead to selfishness, consumption, disaster and destruction. Keenly. Destruction comes to the Earth, which sustains you, which makes life possible.

And so the larger question is why do you have this tension? Is it possible for the individual to make a change in the collective? And it is, my daughter. It is. You, all of you, my children, are a site for Holy influence. The way you live, the example you make, allow for the Holy to come to the present, to be seen and recognized. So, the way you live, the way you perceive is of utmost importance. For the collective can change when the individuals change. And there are some individuals who rise up as great examples of the sacred love, which brings unity and restoration and health and wholeness to the people. There are those who rise up as great leaders and speakers to reveal that the individual can indeed effect the masses. But what if you are not such a one as this? What if you are a one of many? My children, indeed you are one of many. And I shall tell you something about the Sacred and the way it is coming to your day and age. The Sacred is coming in a multiplicity of manifestations. In small circles of influence the Holy comes. And I tell you, the people are gathering in these circles of influence. These peoples are gathering with Holy intention, for they seek the Holy. They seek the Holy. And in these small circles they gather and their yearning, their holy light, is invigorated. There is a glow upon their sacred ember. And so their effect reverberates into culture.

Will there be singular people who rise up? It will take place. But the multiplicity is to be celebrated. Because if there is a singular voice it will be misunderstood and misapplied. It will once again become a single way by which people are judged, a standard by which people are measured. So, I tell you, the Holy comes in multiplicity. And what the people will realize is that there is a common theme among the circles of influence, a common concern. So, the many circles will be both individual and unified. And this is the Holy Way. It is the Holy Way.

So, my daughter, how can you influence the collective? It is through the small circles. Through the small circles that can unite and merge then separate. Is this not the description of existence in the Holy? Be then a small circle of influence and see and resonate with the message of the other small circles. Share perceptions and become a force within society the likes of which has been unknown in history. There is no comparison, my daughter, no comparison for unification through multiplicity. What influence could such a movement have? Do you see it spreading across the cultures? Do you see it, my daughter? In many languages and traditions. Do you see it? A unified goal of health and wholeness and peace. And where shall it be centralized, my daughter, but in the Earth! In the Earth, which gave rise to all life that you understand and see.

**Diane:** Is that why we are feeling such a vibration from the Earth now? Is that why we're feeling a flow of energy from the Earth now?

**The Messenger:** Yes. The Earth cries out. Not only because the Earth needs healed but because the Earth heals. My children, you need only lie upon the ground to know that the Earth can heal. My children, you can be healed by dirt. You can be healed by that which you do not see life in. But it is the sustenance of all life. So, the Earth cries out for the Earth has healing to give, but the Earth needs attention, needs a change of awareness so that the people can understand that the Earth is life. The Earth gives life. And there is great wisdom in the Earth. Great wisdom. So, in the strands of the Braided Way there are traditions that honor the Earth, that understand that the Earth resonates with holy energy. The Earth is a living organism that shelters you and allows you to exist for your existence has risen out of the Earth's protection. For I tell you, the

Earth has a membrane that protects you from the utter cold of space. The Earth has a membrane. It can be penetrated. But my children, it is dissolving. This Holy membrane is dissolving. So, the people must honor the Earth, which formed this membrane, to understand that the Earth gives life.

Does the Earth speak? I tell you, my children, the Earth speaks in a language that is easy to perceive. So, the Earth cries out to the people, does it not? And the Spirit cries out with the Earth, for I tell you, the Earth embodies Spirit. Spirit is woven into the Earth. For the Earth is the result of the Great Release that is the beginning. And so the Earth is of holy materials. And, my children, you are made of the same materials. You are all made of star dust. You are all made of holy substance, that which was given for life to exist. Would you then destroy the very elements of your existence?

So, my daughter, to answer your question, yes. When you open the Earth, when you reach down into the Earth, be ready to receive. Be ready to receive insight, energy and love. It is the nature of the Earth to give. There is abundant generosity in the universe, my children. Abundant generosity. It surrounds you, this generosity. How shall you receive a gift but with a heart-felt thank you. And does not receiving gifts make you want to give? Give in return, then, my children. Do not simply take.

Be agents of healing, then, not only for each other, but for the Earth. Be an influence of sacred awareness so the people will understand that life comes from the Earth, healing comes from the Earth, for Spirit dwells within the Earth.

## CHAPTER 7

# Death and the Life of the Soul

*The book group met on May 23, 2010, and we talked a long time about the topics that had been covered in our wisdom sessions. Then we noted that one topic that had not been touched upon was life after death. We discussed the basic need we have to know something of the afterlife as a way to guide our daily lives. I then entered the oracle state, and to no great surprise, the topic of the lesson was on death and the life of the soul.*

I SEE YOU, MY CHILDREN. I see you. We shall speak of the clouds and the rain drops. We shall speak of the dew and the mist. We shall speak of the soul. We shall speak of life and death, for this is the lesson you have requested.

My children, to explain the end of life, I must explain the spiritual energy and the soul. And to explain spiritual energy and the soul, I must speak of the collection or congealing of Spirit and the layers of awareness. I must speak then, also, of self awareness and holy awareness.

## How the Soul Enters the Body

How does a soul come into a body? There are many ways that this takes place. The process is quite organic and not entirely systematic. I have spoken of souls as stars and lights, but we must change the metaphor for this lesson. Let us speak instead of the clouds and the rain. Indeed. My children, the heavens are like a cloud. But it is a cloud that surrounds you; it is not only in the sky. And the cloud is a collecting place of Spirit. See, then, the mist of the cloud as Spirit. And within the mist there is motion. And, my children, the Spirit collects and congeals as water droplets collect.

See, then, a cloud of Spirit surrounding you, and the fine mist of Spirit washes over the Earth and soaks into the fields and the animals and the insects. And within the mist, there are droplets of awareness, and the droplets soak into the people to give souls awareness. The droplets come from all directions, for the cloud is all around you, even beneath you in the Earth. See, then, rising from the Earth, falling from the sky, sweeping all around you: droplets and mist of Spirit.

On the soul level, the cloud is the mist of Spirit, and a soul is a droplet of mist that has congealed. Thus, the origin of the soul is the mist of cloud around you. The field of spiritual energy that surrounds you, my children, is indeed a cloud of mist.

So, one may ask, What is the origin of the soul? Shall we also ask, What is the origin of a raindrop? It is the cloud. And what is the origin of the cloud? It is moisture in the atmosphere. So it is with the soul.

How does the mist differ from the droplet? This distinction, my children, must be addressed on a spiritual level. In the mist of Spirit, there are droplets. The droplets are larger than the mist, for the droplets are formed when the mist congeals. In the congealing of Spirit, there is awareness. So, the droplets have layers of awareness, as pearls have layers. See, then, that the droplets of Spirit are like rain drops with layers. Pearl drops, shall we call them. These pearl drops of layers are like hail stones that accumulate layers in the cloud, but a pearl is much more elegant than a hail stone. So, we shall mix metaphors to allow for the soul to be a pearl drop of water in the clouds of Spirit.

The pearl drops have awareness. You may see them as souls in the Holy. Some of these souls may choose to enter bodies before they are born. The timing of this entrance is important to the people, but we shall not address this concern at this time. Let us simply say a droplet is drawn into the body before the infant is separated from the waters of the womb. This is the way a pearl drop of Spirit or soul enters a body, but there are other ways Spirit enters a body.

## The Souls of Creatures

Let us turn to creatures of all sizes and types, for all contain spiritual energy from the mist. When a creature is forming and ready to be born, there is an inhale, and the mist enters the creature. So, there is Spirit in the ant. There is Spirit in the bird. There is Spirit in the dog. There is Spirit in the bee, but there is not self awareness. And what happens to the Spirit in the bee when the bee is killed in the frost? The Spirit disseminates into the Holy as water evaporates into a cloud. Is there any retention of being a bee? It is only slight, only slight. My children, when the wolf is born, there is an inhalation of Spirit. And if the wolf falls to starvation, what becomes of the Spirit of the wolf but that it disseminates into the Holy as water evaporates into a cloud. And is there retention of awareness? Yes, but very little self awareness.

Self awareness develops with the congealing of Spirit. The ant, the bee, the bird, all have sacred awareness—that is natural awareness of being connected to a larger whole. However, it is self awareness that distinguishes the human experience from the other creatures, and it distinguishes the soul from the mist. It is a mistake to see a direct hierarchy of spirit, as if a soul must begin as an ant then move up the chain of being to the bee, bird, wolf and human. This is a nursery rhyme orientation of the Holy. No, the Holy enters all beings and all beings are precious, and there is no linear order of importance.

Having said that, I will also add that living moments are one way Spirit congeals. Thus, the moments of the bee do indeed allow the Spirit to congeal into a small droplet, shall we say. However, there is not a systematic process from the bee to the bird, etc., which allows the droplet of the bee to expand through the chain of being until it reaches the human. Instead, a human may receive a soul directly from the mist, just as the ant does.

So, the living moments of a creature act as a catalyst for Spirit. Indeed, moments of living allow Spirit to congeal, so layers of awareness begin to collect through living moments. However, living is not the only way a soul accumulates layers of awareness. In the cloud, droplets of awareness can form without being contained by a living creature. Therefore, souls can develop without living a life. There are many variations, my children. Many variations. Just as a seed can grow in many different types of soil, so too can a soul develop in many different environments.

## The Soul of the Human Being

My children, when a human being is being formed, Spirit enters the body in several ways. One way has intention, for a droplet of pearl may volunteer to enter a life, and in the droplet there is self awareness. Does this mean the raindrop is not made of the same substance as the water that has evaporated from the insect and the wolf? No, it is all of water; it is all of water. But the raindrop is a collection of water that has cohered together into a droplet. Yes. So it is with a soul, my children. And what becomes of the soul in the living body through a lifetime but that another layer is added to it. So, it is that a soul, a pearl drop of Spirit, adds a layer of awareness through the living moments of your existence.

Now, there are other ways a soul enters a person, for not all people receive a raindrop or a soul that is fully formed. There are times that the person breathes in Spirit as an insect or wolf, and suddenly there is new awareness in the Holy for the collection of Spirit coalesces through the mind and experience of the person. Thus, as the body grows, so, too, does the soul. Does this mean that new souls are born? Does this mean that mist comes into a person and coalesces as a raindrop? Yes. My children, awareness is being born in the Holy and developing in the Holy at all times. It is the purpose of living. So, indeed, a new soul can be born in and through a human being. The mist enters the body and a droplet congeals. Once a droplet is formed, there is both self awareness and sacred awareness.

## Young and Old Souls

And here we come to the idea of the old soul and the young soul, which are terms that refer to a person's spiritual maturity. But I tell you, it is not as simple as saying the person's soul that comes from the mist is young while a person's soul that come from a full droplet is old. There are times that the person of the mist exhibits the awareness of the ancients. And there are times that the person with the soul that is fully formed exhibits behaviors of the immature and the self absorbed. It is a dynamic, my children, a dynamic between the life experience of the body and the awareness of the soul. Now, most often the full and complete droplet indeed comes in the body and exhibits an immediate awareness of soul that is deep and abiding—behaviors you would describe as an old soul. And most often a soul from the mist indeed would be a young soul. The young soul, however, does not have to be a self absorbed soul. A young soul can also be a playful soul, a soul of curiosity and delight and generosity.

## Summary of the Cloud Image

So, see, my children, a cloud surrounding you even in the Earth. And see droplets of water coming into your living bodies. See also the mist that comes into all living things, even the trees and the grasses of the field collect dew from the cloud of Spirit. Dew collects in the living moments of the Earth, and what is dew but a droplet of water? All life enhances the awareness of the Sacred.

The image of the cloud of mist has been useful for our lesson. However, I shall complicate the image, for in the Holy these pearl drops or souls can disseminate into the cloud, but retain a sense of Self. Thus, in the Holy, it is easier to say that a soul is a droplet of water in the ocean. A droplet can sense and know the entire ocean, even as it retains a sense of self as a droplet. So, there are limitations to the cloud of mist metaphor, just as there are limitations to all metaphors.

## A Soul in Life

You may wonder why a droplet of Spirit [or soul] in the body of the human would not retain the awareness of the cloud.

In other words, why does an individual forget the life of the soul before incarnation? In the experience of living the understanding of the Whole is difficult to retain, so there is a dominating sense of individual self. This sense of the isolated self is of the mind, not of the soul. Your common or outer experience of life is that the droplet of your soul feels disconnected from the cloud. This is the perception of the mind and body. But the soul or droplet has memory of the Whole, so the sense of the Whole becomes the sense of your soul not the sense of the mind. And in life one must train the mind to accept the sense of unity known on the soul level. The way of sacred awareness is to bring the sensibility of the cloud into the mind and body. Yes, bringing the awareness of the cloud into the moments of being allows for sacred awareness. But I tell you, the individuality that the body brings is a part of the development of the soul. Here we find ourselves in a paradox, in an irony: A soul that knows the Whole comes into the body and feels individuality reigning supreme in experience. Then, it is only through spiritual discipline that the awareness of the Whole returns. The struggle of the individual soul to return to awareness of the Whole enhances sacred awareness and adds a layer to the soul. Thus, there is a purpose to individuality, but the purpose is only fulfilled when individuality is released to the sacred awareness of unity. Do you see the complexity and beauty of the situation?

## Death

Finally, we come to the original question, for what becomes of the awareness of self at the end of your days, my children, is the question posed to us today. And the answer has variations. I have drawn a distinction for you between the spirit and the soul and the mind. The spirit is the living breath and energy. It is the mist of the cloud. It brings animation to you. The soul is the spiritual consciousness, the awareness of the Self with a capital "S"—the Sacred Self. The soul is the droplet of congealed mist. The mind is an organ of perception, a storehouse of stimulation. When life begins, the droplet of soul enters the person, and spiritual energy also enters to give animation and life. At the time of death, my children, the spirit disseminates into the Holy as water evaporates into the cloud. The mind goes dormant as an organ without energy, and the soul remains. The soul seeks unification with the Holy, the place of origin. And I tell you, the sense of Self has been strengthened through the experience of living, but it is Self with a capital S. It is a selfless Self.

## Memory after Death

Now, this you will not want to hear, but memory is different in soul than it is in mind. At death, my children, memory is altered for mind is absent. Memory becomes soul memory. It is highly emotional. Very imagistic. And what is retained most prominently are the bonds of love. For these things are Holy. The bonds of love. The emotions of living become the awareness of the soul. And so a layer is added to the pearl drop. A layer of many layers.

## The Soul After Death

At the time of death, does the Soul remain among the living? This varies. It is in some ways a choice: not a choice that is made of the mind, a choice that is made of the soul, a feeling of emotion and of relationship, a sense of responsibility to loved ones. There is often a pull to the soul, and often the soul is pulled to remain for the sake of sharing and relationship. And most souls also feel the pull to the Whole to return to the place of origin, return to the cloud, shall we say. So, many souls choose to honor the love of relationships among the living while also heeding the pull of the Whole. This allows for a dynamic interplay between the Holy and the living.

## Reincarnation

Is it possible for the droplet to come back into a body? It is indeed. Why? For the experience of adding a layer of awareness. For my children, awareness is a beautiful thing in the Holy, and it is made especially uniquely in the human being. Certainly, there is a selfless Self in the wolf, in the dog, in the cat, in the dolphin, in the whale. But they are different than the selfless Self in a human being. The selfless Self in the human being is a great and treasured awareness.

Is it possible for the soul of a wolf to be reincarnated as a human being? Certainly. The soul of the wolf would be a small droplet that could indeed be absorbed, with other sacred energies, into a human being, forming a larger droplet of Spirit.

Why doesn't a person remember the lives of the past? As I have explained, memory in the soul is different from memory in the mind. Soul memory is imagistic and emotional. Thus, there is not a full forgetting of previous lives; it is simply that the memory is on the soul level and not the mind level. Having said this, there is a purpose to not remembering previous incarnations because it allows the soul to be fully present in the moments of living. An entire lesson could be brought on this topic.

## Errant Souls

Now, my children, there are times that a soul does not wish to be reunited in the Whole. There is a resistance and a clinging to self. Such souls travel about often among the living in order to retain and impose a sense of self. It is a limited self, certainly. Such are troubled souls, my children, troubled souls. And they are all around you. They are sometimes parasites that feed upon the weaknesses of the living. For a weakness that is retained and not given to the Holy often becomes a place of clutching for self. Thus, spiritual un-health can leave one a victim to errant souls.

Because of the errant souls around you, it is always important for those who communicate with the spiritual messengers to test the source of information. There are many errant souls who would provide information that you wish to know in order to further establish a sense of self. You must see, then, that there is deception within the spiritual realm. Not all spiritual messengers are selfless and mature. Some messengers are errant or troubled souls, providing partial perspectives and deceptive answers. Always test the information from spiritual messengers to be sure the messenger is a selfless Self, a mature spirit.

## Summary and Conclusions

So, this is how I explain to you today the process of receiving soul and the process after death, when the Spirit dissolves into the Holy, the mind goes dormant and the soul is retained as awareness. Now, my children, when you live a life that cultivates sacred awareness of the soul, you provide your soul with a layer of awareness that is a blessing. And this soul takes with it from the life vivid emotion and development of Self, images and ties of love. Cultivate, then, sacred awareness. Cultivate, then, sacred awareness.

But I tell you, when one lives a self-absorbed life without sacred awareness, the soul will often return to the Holy with very little of what you would call memory. Very little. And sometimes the emotion that is carried is counter to the Holy surrender. And there is, shall we say, soul damage. And when the soul returns to the Whole, there is healing. There is healing and embrace and love.

Now, you may wonder does a soul choose to come into a body? As I have said, it is more accurate to say "volunteer" rather than "choose." When there is a call into the Holy for a conscious and aware soul, there is a volunteering. Why would one volunteer? Perhaps it is decided that awareness will be enhanced for this particular droplet. Perhaps it will be decided that healing must take place in this particular droplet. And perhaps it is simply a volunteering out of exuberance and joy, not for learning but for simply giving, simply participating. And this is the most blessed soul.

## Evolution of Sacred Awareness

My children, awareness in the Holy is something that has evolved. This is not what the people wish to know, but it is so. Awareness in the Holy has evolved. The droplets have increased through human experience. This is not to say there was not awareness in the Holy, for there was. But there is a particular type of rain being formed through the human.

## Karma

My children, the idea of karma is in many ways accurate in this framework for the soul can be increased or injured based upon experience and emotion in the living. So, there can be emotion of love and caring and generosity and compassion, and there can be emotion of pain and sorrow and frustration and anger. The emotion informs the soul. And hence, there can be injury to soul that is then brought with the soul into another life. Do you see? So, we shall explain karma as the emotion of the soul, the development of the selfless Self. So, it matters how life is lived and what emotions become dominant in your experience. Live, then, in a way that promotes and cultivates sacred awareness and brings with it generosity, and compassion, and patience, and kindness, and love.

Are there questions?

## QUESTIONS AND ANSWERS

### The Doctrine of the Last Judgment

**Christopher:** The doctrine of the last judgment that is firmly established in Christianity and in Islam is an obstacle because it doesn't jive with what you describe and what you're familiar with. You have a chance to offer a teaching to expand it or recap the story of the last judgment of souls to be condemned forever or to be in heaven forever.

**The Messenger:** The idea of the last judgment is unfortunate. But there are sacred origins for the idea, and it served a function in the human development of sacred awareness. But it is no longer beneficial for what it does is it mandates certain behaviors upon the human and often the creative soul does not respond well to the mandates. The result is guilt, shame and struggle.

So, let us speak first of condemnation, for I tell you, there is no condemnation in the Holy. There is no blame. There is no guilt. There is only love and acceptance. Having said that, as I have explained, there are sometimes souls that wish to

retain self and identity and thus resist surrender to the Wholeness. Sometimes we see these as injured souls, and we reach
out to the injured souls. But there is often a stubborn resistance. These souls can surrender into the Wholeness at any
time, and there is no judgment or condemnation. But, my
children, there is choice. So, these souls may choose to clutch
identity. And there are times, my children, these souls become
darkened through pain and sorrow, and there is an inability
to feel compassion, and they become parasites of souls of the
living. This you may see as evil, but there is still compassion
for the soul that is separated from Wholeness. But, my children, there comes a point where these souls must be received
into the Holy. There is not condemnation, but there are times
that these souls are brought back to the Holy to be remade
and reformed. Indeed, they are brought back to the void, to
the abyss, to the place of beginnings, not for judgment but for
healing, for reformation.

Errant souls fear the loss of self, so they clutch to self.
The irony is that if they lose self to the Holy, they receive a
selfless Self, a Self beyond self. It is a further irony that if they
clutch to self to the point of injury to other souls, they can
be sent to the abyss to be, shall we say, recycled into spiritual
energy. Thus, the errant souls fear the void, the deep and the
abyss. If you encounter an errant soul, send them to the light.
You can tell them that their options are the light or the abyss.
There are some people among you who feel a call to assist
the errant and lost souls. It can be a deep and honorable call
and purpose.

What I have explained is the only "hell" in the Holy. There
is no condemnation or damnation in the Holy, but there is acceptance and reformation.

So, my children, the sacred awareness of this reformation or recycling of the errant soul was brought into human awareness at a time that laws were being made for acceptable behaviors, and quickly the idea of law brought with it the ideas of justice, punishment and judgment. Do you see? The sacred awareness was simply brought into human awareness at a time when the Sacred was seen as providing law and punishment. But I tell you, the Holy is generous and compassionate. It does not offer judgment but healing and wholeness, healing and wholeness to all souls, to all souls: young or ancient, mature or immature, selfless or self absorbed.

Another inspiration for Hell is the trash heap, where refuse can burn and decay. At times, bodies of enemies were thrown into the trash heap at the edge of the city. Hence, the idea of a burning Hell. I tell you, there is no trash heap in the Holy. There is no throw-away in the Holy. Nobody is thrown aside, no soul is left to decay. No, all is embraced in the Holy, and if it is not embraced, it is recycled into renewed Spirit. This is the nature of the Holy, my children. So, do not look for a trash heap of burning souls in the Holy, for there is no such place. It is time for the human consciousness to grow beyond this image of judgment and waste.

Yes, my children, the ways of society always influence the understanding of the Holy. This is why the understanding of the Holy must be allowed to change as civilization changes. For the human awareness evolves. And I tell you, spiritual awareness evolves. Let the two evolve together, my children, and be blessed.

**Christopher:** The other unfortunate teaching is the teaching of an eternal life and an eternal damnation that things stop and that -

**The Messenger:** There is no eternal damnation. No eternal damnation. No. There is eternal wholeness and fullness. There are times, my children, that a droplet of soul may indeed dissipate and be absorbed into the Holy as water is absorbed into a cloud, but this is not damnation. No, it is simply absorption into the Whole. And I tell you, it is finally the end of all souls. For the ancient ones among us are souls of great development. They have a light. Indeed they have a light. And I tell you, they finally come to a place where they dissolve of selfless Self into the Whole, and this is seen as a final development into Ultimate Awareness. You must see the wisdom of it. If the release of self is Sacred, then the final step of release is a complete surrender to the Whole. The most developed souls willingly surrender to the Whole to be embraced into the All.

But do not fear the annihilation or damnation of the soul. You all have a place in the Holy. You all have a seat, my children, a seat, a place, a room, a space. A mother droplet, shall we say, a pool of the Holy. You are tadpoles –

**Sandy:** What about –

**The Messenger:** - of water in the pool of the Holy. You were saying?

**Sandy:** Sorry. I was just wondering about the other end of the spectrum. I was rock climbing once and I could swear I could feel the rock was alive.

**The Messenger:** Yes.

## Spirit in Rock and All Things

**Sandy:** When I hold my pipe [Native American prayer pipe], I have this emotional spiritual connection –

**The Messenger:** Yes.

**Sandy:** It is a living thing. So how does that fit in?

**The Messenger:** Rocks can speak. The mist is in all things. The Holy is in all things. It is the Living Breath. It is the living energy. It is in the rock. It is in the grass. It is in the soil. It is in the crust of the Earth. It is in the atmosphere. It is in the cosmos.

There is awareness in the Holy, even in the rock. And there are ways that this awareness is collected in pockets. And when you come upon a pocket, my daughter, you will feel the awareness. It is not awareness as you know it. It is sacred energy that is collected. Here we can not use the image of the droplet, but we can use the image of the mist, the mist in creation. There are tunnels and veins in creation. Indeed, in the Earth there are pockets of swirling energy.

And the sacred energy of the pipe, my daughter, is brought forth through the sharing between you and the Sacred around you. The pipe becomes a funnel and conduit. There are other sacred objects that people imbue with Holy energy: crosses, effigies, necklaces, jewelry. Indeed, indeed. Matter collects spiritual energy. Does this make sense to you?

**Sandy:** Yes. It does.

**Christopher:** I pray that, that we all would send a prayer to that place, this damnation, Hell, that you have said does not exist in the Holy. That story has caused great damage here on Earth, and I ask that you send forth now more assistance into the easing of that teaching, a release from it…I feel this deeply. There's much pain caused by this teaching, and I make this prayer for that teaching to be dissolved.

**The Messenger:** The teaching will be dissolved only when the people understand that there is not control in the Holy, and thus, there should not be control among the human. For the teaching of damnation evolves out of a need to control, a need to shape. But I hear your heart, my son, I hear your heart, and I know your compassion, and so we shall send a prayer for those under the influence of this teaching of oppression and judgment that they may feel a release and a relief, for the Sacred accepts and receives and does not judge.

## Eternal Ties

**Diane:** Could you speak of those who have died and we feel their energy and presence with us?

**The Messenger:** Yes.

**Diane:** Would that be a way to help us to understand about the fact that this concept of damnation is not true? When we feel presences of people and we feel the beauty…

**The Messenger:** Certainly, my daughter, you feel the presence of the soul that is tied by relationality, awareness of sacredness, compassion. Yes, the soul often remains to honor these ties and to reveal their endurance. Such a soul reveals that all is well; all is as it should be. Let there not be so much sorrow, but let there be love that endures through all things, love that is eternal that stretches forth and into the Holy. The ties that bind, my daughter, can be eternal. And yes, does it not reflect the opposite of the teaching of damnation, that there is acceptance and love and peace.

## Guiding Errant Souls

Realize also, my daughter, there is experience of spiritual darkness, and see how this is led to the idea of damned souls. For these we would call errant souls, the ones clutching for identity. They are not damned, however.

**Diane:** Is there a way to help them?

**The Messenger:** Oh, yes.

**Diane:** And is there a way in our own lives that we can point the way, very much like the whales that were turned around to move back into the sea?

**The Messenger:** There are many who feel the call to aid the errant souls. For there are people among you, my children, who actually *see* these souls and feel the call to guide them to wholeness. There are also those who are troubled by these souls, but they may not have the call to guide them to wholeness. But there is indeed a calm you can bring to the beached soul, a calm and a turning towards the depths. Indeed, my daughter, indeed, indeed. And the Holy is there as the ocean is there, to receive the beached soul.

## Dual Awareness

**Christopher:** In thinking about our circle here of spiritual friends, we often have the experience that we are united but that individuality is supported and nurtured. We are each strengthened to be ourselves by being in the circle, and there is also a sense that we are one. You've been speaking of the soul as a singular entity, and what we are experiencing in the circle is how we share soul at another level. Would you speak to us about this?

**The Messenger:** Yes.

**Christopher:** The place where the souls are one yet multiple in their individuality, yet they love each other.

**The Messenger:** One and multiple at the same time. It is difficult to understand but it is true. In the Holy we are One and in the Holy we have purpose. I would not say individuality, but I would say awareness. So, your souls, my children, are a part of the whole and they have memory of merging and they have desire to merge, and when you come together with sacred intention, I see you merge, I see you become a droplet. I see you become an orb. It is beautiful to behold when the many become aware of the One and merge, and there is both awareness of the Self and awareness of the Whole. A dual awareness. And I tell you, this dual awareness is what I know in the Holy. It is indeed what I know. It is awareness of selfless Self and awareness of the Whole. And it is beautiful. And it is what you feel and what you sense in your sacred moments. So, there is awareness of the selfless Self and there is awareness of love and compassion and acceptance and mutuality and connection. Indeed.

**Diane:** As human beings in spirit and soul, it feels like we're evolving into another space where we can become aware of this understanding of somebody else's feeling and thought particularly those who are working in the same circle. Is this true, and are we evolving to a point where we can understand this in more depth?

## Evolving Awareness

**The Messenger:** I have two answers for you. One is that the awareness of the Whole has been known among the human for generations upon generations upon generations. And in this way let us say that it is constant. But I will also say that awareness of the Sacred evolves as the human awareness evolves, and so it is constantly altered and changing. So your circumstance, your situation both as individuals and as a collective provides a new opportunity for Holy awareness.

So, awareness of the unification of all things, awareness of the soul, sensibilities of the other has been around since the dawn of self awareness among the human, and yet here you are living it anew. So, it is both eternal and constant and always changing.

It is not a simple answer.

There is much talk of a new awareness among the people, for they wish there to be sudden development of soul within their lifetimes. But they must realize that they should honor the development of soul in the past and celebrate it and know it. The new cannot come without an awareness of the ancient. And the new will not come upon the people as a sudden flash of lightening but as a bathing of rain to a season.

## Origin of Matter and Soul

**Sandy:** I'm a little confused about the origin of the souls. There was the release, and I thought all things came from the release and that's where the origin of the mist, the raindrops were. Yet you said new souls are born. So, can you enlighten me on this a little more?

**The Messenger:** Yes. First of all let me say that it is mysterious. Even in the Holy it is not understood. It is accepted. But I shall try to explain to you. All things, indeed began with the release. All possibilities began with the release. But I tell you, my daughter, in combinations of elements there are new substances and the same is true of Spirit. So, if all things began in the burst of the release, you must see that light and energy is the origin of substance but the substance had to cool, the substance had to combine in order to become other substances.

Do you see? Do you see that hydrogen combined with other substances? The origin of all matter, then, began with the release, but it is gathered in different ways at different temperatures in different places in different combinations. So it is with soul, with Spirit. It began at the release, but it is combined in new ways. You may see it as the mist. You may see it as the light. The mist and the light. The Holy is in all things, even the Earth. But the mist can congeal into a droplet in the Earth and rise to the surface. And the mist can congeal in the sky and fall to the surface. And the mist can congeal in the body. So the substance of soul is from the beginning, but the birth of soul takes place continually and the release of soul also takes place, for the ancient ones release, finally, to become Ultimate Awareness.

So, shall you see the mist around you and droplets congealing in the Earth and the air, in the sky, entering into bodies and sometimes the midst itself comes into a body and congeals. And see the droplets going to the cloud, congealing with other droplets to become a family of droplets, and see the droplets rise finally and disseminate into the cloud itself. There is a constant congealing and adding to awareness.

Does this make sense to you?

**Sandy:** I think so.

**The Messenger:** There was not a certain number of souls at the beginning. In fact, the whole idea, the whole possibility of soul did not come forth at the beginning. The possibility, let's say, was there but the awareness evolved. This is complicated. Ultimate Awareness was present even before the beginning. Individual awareness, selfless Self awareness has evolved through and because of the release. You are a part of this process.

## Closing

My children, I must close for Michael's energy is waning. I shall close with telling you to be mystified. Seek to be the mist. Be mystified! Surrender self to the mist. Do not worry that you will disseminate and evaporate into non-awareness. No. Be mystified, my children. Combine your mist. Surrender your sense of self. It is the mystery of the Sacred. You are mist and you are droplets. You are both.

I shall say something to Michael, for he is in a place of frustration. And the emotion he forms in his soul can be eternal so he must be aware that frustration can be released. His sacred task is upon him. His sacred task is upon him, and he worries that he will not accomplish it for he is in the middle of his existence. There are so many demands on him, and there seems to be a lifetime of work to get the oracles out to the people. So, there is a sense of urgency upon him. And I would say, do not be afraid, my son, do not be afraid. Pace yourself. Pace yourself and cultivate sacred awareness as you write about sacred awareness. Be mystified, my son, be mystified. Go to the Earth and surrender for you are to speak for Grandmother [the Earth].

Be mystified, my children. Be the mist of spirit among the people.

## CHAPTER 8

# Spirit and the Earth

*Note: Many of us in the book group were concerned about the Earth, and we had not received any guidance about the sacred nature of the Earth. So, in an e-mail, I suggested that we all focus on the Earth for the wisdom session scheduled for April 18, 2010. When we gathered on that date, the following lesson came through me. It was an astounding lesson that left us all amazed and awed.*

M<small>Y</small> CHILDREN, I see you. I see you. My children, the time has come to see the incarnation of Spirit as Spirit itself and not to see the physical matter as less than the spiritual presence, for we shall see they are woven together and interdependent; indeed, Spirit and matter are of the same origins and material.

There is no wisdom in viewing the sky as Spirit and the Earth as matter. It leads to a false distinction, which devalues the Earth. For the Earth is of Spirit and Light.

## The Origins of Spirit and Matter: Light and Substance

At the beginnings of beginnings, there was darkness and substance, and the Spirit of the Holy dwelt there. From the darkness and substance came the eruption of birth, and there was light and space. But the light was so bright that life as you know it could not begin. The light had to cool and congeal, and there was matter, but within the matter is the light. You must see that the matter is the light, for all things were light. Accept, then, that the Earth is light, and know that this light is the Light of Spirit. The Earth is the eruption of origins, cooled for the possibility of living, still warm from the fires of creation.

## Spirit Within the Earth

It is assumed that the Spirit of Life comes from above and flows down onto the Earth. I tell you, this is not so. You must see that the Spirit of Life, the Holy, permeates all things and does not come from above but comes from beyond, through and within: beyond, through and within.

You must see that the Holy permeates all things. You must see that the Holy sweeps through the universe, but also abides in the Earth. Yes, I tell you, the Spirit is gathered in the Earth, for there are spiritual veins in the Earth. There are pores and there are pockets in the Earth. And the Spirit gathers in the Earth, spins through the Earth. Certainly, the Spirit pervades all things, but there are veins in the Earth where the Spirit gathers and sweeps and travels.

And, my children, the people with spiritual perception can feel these veins, and they can feel the pockets where these veins emerge to the surface. They are Holy areas, sacred places where the Spirit swells and swirls. And the Spirit comes and goes in and through the Earth, comes and goes, my children, into the cosmos and back. It is the spiritual energy of creation. So, if it were visual you would see veins coursing through the cosmos and some entering Earth as if the Earth in the cosmos were a heart of many hearts, and the veins go from heart to heart and organ to organ, and the energy courses through the universe. It is much larger than you think, and Earth is connected to an expansive system, is woven into this system. So, what happens to the Earth happens to all of the universe.

What happens when a heart collapses in a great body of many hearts? Certainly, the body of the universe will continue without this heart, but there will be a lack, an incredible lack. For the Spirit that flows through this heart carries precious, precious awareness. What is the awareness of this heart of the cosmos? The awareness is of Self.

## Awareness in the Earth

Self awareness, my children. Do you think you are the only creatures with self awareness? My children, the Earth has self awareness. Those who speak to the Earth know this. And it is the gift to the universe, this self awareness. So, you may wonder, how is it the Earth itself has self awareness? My children, it is the awareness of the Holy, but it comes to a unique life in the Earth. The Holy is embodied in the Earth. Thus, the awareness of the Holy is within the Earth, and this awareness is shaped by the Earth.

With this awareness in the Earth there is motivation and action and generosity and a will for balance. It is the Holy in the Earth, the Spirit in the matter, the Light in the substance.

## Life from the Earth

Now, I shall turn things upside down for you. I shall be heretical to your thinking. For it is believed that the creation of life on Earth came from the Heavens, came from above Earth, came from outside of Earth. My children, this is backwards. The creation of life came from within the Earth.

So, let us see that the Spirit of the Holy is in all things and sweeps through the universe. Certainly. But let us see that this Spirit of the Holy is collected in this planet. There are other planets in which the Holy collects, but let us concern ourselves with your Earth. The Holy abides in this planet. And with the Spirit of the Holy is awareness. So, the Spirit of the Holy within this Earth presented the will to create. The creative Spirit of the universe dwelt in the Earth, and the Earth collected and directed this creative Spirit, and there was life. I tell you, the will for life came through the Earth itself. And this life began with the smallest of elements, my children, the smallest of elements. From the gasses of the Earth, from the breath of the Earth, from the expulsions of the Earth came the atmosphere, the membrane of protection.

My children, do you think it came simply by chance? Do you think it came from a will above? My children, it came from the Holy awareness within. And so the Earth began to harbor life in waters, in cells, and the secret to life is the membrane, the protective breath of the Earth.

The Earth itself has a membrane. So, should cells not have a membrane? My children, it was the secret of life as you know it. So, cells with membranes multiplied and became complex. And the membrane and the cells began to interact with the environment, with the Earth. Do you see? And the interaction brought forth life. The interaction brought forth complexity. The interaction brought forth adaptation for existence. My children, do you see that evolution came from the interaction of cells with the environment? It was a discourse, my children, a discourse. So, from the Earth there arose life, and in the interaction with the Earth there came variety. And from this life, Spirit is magnified, and even generated. Do you see? Do you see?

So, the plan for life, the design of species, the variety of existence became through the Spirit of Life in the Earth.

So, my children, I have turned you upside down, and I tell you, you are indeed made in the image of God. But see, the image is not only from above. It is also below. From the very substance of your bodies you are made of Light, but Light cooled to Earth temperature and image. You are made of Earth. And my children, the lessons of existence are seen in the Earth, for the Earth is compassionate, the Earth is generous, the Earth is selfless. My children, the Earth seeks balance. You must see it. All spiritual wisdom is reflected in the Earth, for the Spirit abides in the Earth.

## When Humanity Turned Away from the Earth

So, the Holy ones have always looked to the Earth to read the signs of the Spirit, and I tell you, the signs are there. Why? Because the Spirit is in the Earth. Now, my children, this knowledge has existed amongst the people since the beginnings of human consciousness, but there came a time when the Earth was seen as nothing but dead rock. And so civilizations arose that saw themselves higher than the Earth, higher than the substance of life. And, therefore, they viewed the Spirit as above and outside of Earth. I tell you, my children, it is a move that changed everything among the people and for the Earth. The Earth teaches cooperation and generosity, and the people no longer live these lessons. And now the awareness of the Spirit within the Earth has been so limited among the people it is almost forgotten.

There is very little dialogue now between the Earth and the human, and the wisdom of the Earth has not been heard for many generations.

Listen to me well, my children, listen to me well. The truth of the matter is that the Spirit of the Holy is both outside and inside the Earth. The Spirit of the Holy courses through the Earth and through the universe.

So, both perspectives are actually correct. The Spirit is above the Earth, surrounding the Earth, but I tell you, the Spirit is also in the Earth, in the very substance of the Earth. For if you look at your own bodies, my children, where is life? Where is the life? Is it not in the very flesh? Is it not in the very bones? Is there not life in your substance? In the very cells of your bodies? My children, there is life in the Earth as well, coursing through the Earth. And the Earth has healing properties. Indeed, you can be healed by dirt, my children: by the very dust beneath your feet.

So, the ways of worshipping with the Earth have nearly been lost, almost completely. For the people who worshipped the sky thought that the people who worshipped the Earth worshipped dead matter, were lacking in understanding. My children, the people who worshipped the Earth were not worshiping dead substance. They were worshiping the Spirit in the Earth and of the Earth. And so it was seen that those who used and utilized the spiritual power of the Earth must be engaged in a lesser power then those who utilize the spiritual powers of the sky. And so those who utilized the spiritual powers of the Earth were seen as magicians and witches. I tell you, my children, it is the same spiritual power. It is the same, but it comes with a different language, for the spiritual energy that comes through the Earth speaks differently than the spiritual energy that sweeps through the cosmos. For, my children, Spirit is informed by the matter in which it is embodied. So, you inform the Spirit of your bodies through your lives, and the Earth informs the Spirit of the Holy as it is embodied. So, you must see that to be whole beings you must understand that the Spirit is both above and below. And you must understand that the Spirit below has a great deal to teach you. And you must also understand, when the Spirit is wrung out of the Earth, life is wrung out of your bodies.

My children, this is one area in which the Braided Way can save humanity and the planet. There are still strands of traditions that worship with the Earth. There are still ceremonies, which allow you to commune with and learn from the Earth. There are still people to teach how to see the Holy in both the sky and the Earth. Do you see that these strands can strengthen the braid of life? My children, retrieve these strands and become aware of the Holy in the Earth. Restore the lessons of community and generosity, of relationship and compassion, which the Holy teaches through the Earth.

## The Earth Generates Life and Spirit

There is a great deal more to tell you, my children. Let us continue with your re-orientation to the Earth. You must also know that the Earth is a generator. It is not a dead rock in space. It is a generator of life and the substance of life. And I tell you, where life is generated, Spirit is generated. Thus, the Earth generates Spirit. It is a mistake to think that Spirit comes from outside of matter, for Spirit comes forth also through matter. So it is with the Earth.

My children, do you know the sediments of the Earth do not come from above? The soil of the Earth is not the dust of the cosmos coming down to settle. No. The layers come from the Earth itself. The Earth is a living organism. And around the Earth is a membrane, which protects, sustains and feeds life. Without the membrane the light of creation would burn you to pieces and the space of creation would swallow you up. So the atmosphere of the Earth, the membrane, protects you and gives you your very breath.

I tell you, my children, the membrane of the Earth is in jeopardy. It is indeed in jeopardy. And what shall the Earth be without its membrane? It shall be like a body without its flesh, vulnerable to all forms of invasion and disease. And without the flesh and membrane, my children, there is no life.

## Wisdom in the Earth

And I tell you, there is Spirit in the Earth. There is guidance in the Earth. There is wisdom in the Earth. There is healing in the Earth. There is presence in the Earth. There is consciousness in the Earth. How can this be, you wonder? How can this be?

My children, there are a multitude of spiritual presences in the Earth just as there are in the surrounding spaces. Heaven is all around you, even beneath you. So, these presences give guidance and direction and purpose. Indeed, they are of the Earth, and I tell you, there are people among you who are born of the Earth literally. Their souls are from the Earth. And such people have a resonance with the Earth. Such people can feel the earthquake before it comes. Such people weep when the forest is leveled. Such people cry when the water dries up because of use and abuse. My children, there are those among you whose souls begin in the Earth, for the Earth generates.

There was a time these people would be the communicators with the Earth, and to the people they would bring the message, to the people they would explain the balance, to the people they would reveal the secrets hidden in the Earth. For the secrets of survival are hidden in the Earth. The secrets of creation are in the Earth. The secrets of the relationship between you and the Holy is in the Earth. It is all written in the Earth, my children. It is all written in the Earth. Study the Earth and learn all things. Study the Earth, and see that all things in both Spirit and matter are explained and laid out for you as a book is written. Yes. Oh, and my children, listen and you will receive direction from the Earth, teachings from the Earth. I tell you, the language of the Earth is not only written, it is also spoken. Even now the language is there to be discerned. But who reads and who listens to the message of the Earth? And the message is deeper than science can tell. Yes, your own spirit must read the Earth. Yes, all the faculties must be used. The mind and the heart. The eyes and the feel of the fingers. All must be used. For the Earth communicates in so many ways, in so many revelations. You could spend your entire lives reading the stories of the Earth, and they would be lives well spent.

## Living in Balance with the Earth

So, how does humanity learn to live in balance and cooperation with the Spirit of matter? For this is the great matter of our discourse. It is all that truly matters. So, what is the matter with the human awareness that has grown away from the Earth? It has grown away from its origins and grown away from the wisdom and power of living in cooperation with the Spirit of matter.

So, how shall you learn the language of the Earth? How, indeed, shall you learn the language of the Earth, my children? It is a language that is natural to you. So, go to school with the Earth, and you shall learn the language, and behold, just as the languages of your peoples are full of variety so, too, is the language of the Earth. There are some who can feel the language, can feel it seep into their bodies. There are some who witness the messages with the turning of the seasons. There are some who hear the messages in the other creatures of the Earth, for I tell you something, the other creatures of the Earth still understand how to live in relationship with the Earth, and there is dialogue and communication. How else do the birds know where to fly when they migrate? The Earth speaks to them, my children, and they know the language. They read the signs. Indeed.

Experience the ceremonies of worshipping with the Earth. Do not confuse worship with thinking. *Feel* yourselves merge with the Earth, with the cosmos. Learn these ways of increasing your sacred awareness, and see that community strengthens, generosity increases, compassion flows forth, and wasteful consumption is curtailed. I can be no plainer than this. It is my direct plea.

Do you see, my children? The consumption for self must be curtailed through the sacred awareness of the Holy. The ways of society must be informed by the ways of the Earth. The ways of the self must be transformed by the ways of the Holy.

But, my children, as humanity evolved and self consciousness intensified, there was a tendency to ignore relationship with the Earth. Human consciousness grew away from the Earth. So, the human saw development as separation from the Earth, and thus humanity separated itself from the animal and natural, so as to be civilized. And I tell you, this self consciousness began to evolve to a place where it began to denigrate all things that come from body and Earth, until finally self consciousness seems to be a goal in and of itself. And so there is consumption for self in consciousness of self.

Let the way of self consciousness give way to the Ways of sacred awareness. Let there be awareness of the sacred Self, which is connected to all things. Self consciousness must give way to sacred awareness.

So, you are to come to a holy awareness. And the awareness of the Holy demands that you understand your relationship to the Earth, for the Earth shall teach you the lessons of sacred awareness.

So, my children, there is a great turning point among the people. Will the people finally understand that they must care for the Earth and in so doing will the people share a similar care, a similar goal? Will it bring the peoples together? It is a great hope among many. A great hope among many. But I tell you, it will not be successful without the element of Spirit. Without the spiritual connection to the Earth, all activities will be in vain. For the Earth is your origin and from your origin will come the direction. And from the direction will come the awareness. And from the awareness will come the activities. And through the activities there shall come unification. And with unification there shall be peace and restoration. But my children, without the spiritual awareness of the Earth, there is not a full communication with your environment. So, it is of the utmost importance that the people are reminded of the Spirit of the Earth. The Holy is in the Earth, my children. The Holy is in you. The Holy is throughout the universe. The Holy abides within, beyond and through all things.

Are there questions?

## QUESTIONS AND ANSWERS

### A Dream of Earth's Rejuvenation

**Christopher:** The first one is I had a dream that has given me hope for many years, and I'll speak it, and then I ask that you would respond. I'm in a time when the rage against the Earth has stopped, and I can feel that because of the way the atmosphere feels around me. I'm walking on a road with some friends, and life is coming up through the stones, and I look to the river and the rivers are coming back, and it's very moving. And I feel someway I am in that place, and I wish you to speak on that one.

**The Messenger:** You wish me to speak on a new Heaven and a new Earth. But I tell you, the Heavens and the Earth shall not be new but the awareness of the people shall be *re-newed*. It is a great hope, what you see and feel in this dream. It is what you feel that is most important. For what you feel is the connection to the atmosphere and the environment so much so that you can feel the restoration. Yes, it is a good dream. And is it possible for humanity to live such a dream, to come to a place where there is rejuvenation to the point that the atmosphere is thicker and the streams are cleaner? In the Spirit of generosity and creation which sweeps through the cosmos and resonates in your Earth, it is indeed possible. It is the hope of the Holy. So, the Holy will raise up among the people those who speak for the Earth, those who listen to the Earth. Yes. It shall be. It shall be. The question is, will the masses change their behaviors? This is a great question. A great question. For, there is the individual consciousness of a person and there is a mass consciousness of a civilization. And the mass consciousness of a civilization is an unwieldy beast. For in masses, the people can forget their own consciousness. And so they begin to internalize the consciousness of the civilization.

My children, how does the consciousness of a civilization become altered? It is only through the individual consciousness that you bring. So, cleanse your consciousness. Spend time listening to the Earth and teach the language of the Earth to the people, and let the people then begin to alter the awareness of the civilization. It is possible, my children. It is possible. And it is beginning. It is beginning. It is beginning.

But what do I see? What do I see in the near future of the Earth in your relationship to it? I see catastrophe. I, indeed, see catastrophe. Why? The consciousness of the civilizations is slow to change, but change will come. Change indeed will come.

## How The Earth Speaks

**Christopher:** At certain points in life nature comes forth in an unusual way that tells a person their name and why they are here. For example, my experience with the fox or different experiences where nature sees and holds very specifically the identity of the person and mirrors it to that person. I call that the "enchanted land" experience. It's a good way to teach. This is a chance for you to offer a teaching.

**The Messenger:** The Earth speaks in so many ways, in so many ways. Through the growth upon the Earth, through the winds of the Earth, through the rains of the Earth, through the creatures of the Earth, the Earth speaks. And I tell you, there is great wisdom in the Earth. There is indeed consciousness in the Earth. There are spirits in the Earth. So, the Earth speaks. And I tell you, the Earth doesn't simply hold its speech. The Earth speaks continually. And the Earth wishes to speak. And so when there is a person willing to hear, the Earth celebrates. My children, go out into the Earth with an intention and sit quietly, and you will find answers, you will find answers, indeed.

So, the question is, is there a sense of identity for the individual in the Earth? The Earth, like the Holy in all things, can read you. Therefore, the Earth will sometimes tell you what it reads. So, the Earth will understand your spiritual essence just as the Holy understands your spiritual essence outside of the Earth. My children, the Holy is in all things. Therefore, does it not make sense that the Holy would speak through the Earth?

So, it is true that a person's purpose and identity for living can be read by the Earth and through the Earth, and it can be revealed. It is true, my children, and generations have known it. Generations have lived it. So. It is so.

## The Medicine Wheel

**Christopher:** And last, look at the work I did yesterday at the medicine wheel. Please speak on it. The medicine wheel is a way to teach people the language of the Earth.

**The Messenger:** The medicine wheel, my son, is an ancient symbol. It has upon it directions, but it is also a circle because all things and all directions are related. The circle can spin and still those who know the Earth know the directions are oriented in the Earth. And each direction has a different sign, a different magnetism, a different voice. So, it is possible to stand in the center of a medicine wheel and know the direction of all things. And I tell you, in the Holy there is no direction finally; it is a directionless place. It is the Earth that gives you the direction. For as soon as you leave the surface of the Earth and venture out into space, there is no north and south, there is no east and west. And the Holy seems to sweep without the voice and magnetism of the directions. So, it is a way for the Earth to speak to you specifically. It is an orientation to your planet. It is an orientation to the Spirit of your planet. Does this make sense to you?

Christopher: Yes.

The Messenger: So, you are teaching the people to feel, are you not?

Christopher: Yes and to see it and describe the process.

## Natural Disasters and the Earth

Holly: I have a question about the seeming disasters of the Earth of late and the mass extermination of the local humanity. So many of us perceive this with great fear. Is this strictly a balancing? Is this just a neutral event or is it something we need to focus love on to counteract?

The Messenger: Yes. Yes, to all of it. The Earth is an organism, and the Earth moves. There is energy in the Earth. And the energy in the cosmos affects the Earth. The energy of the stars and planets affects the Earth. The moon affects the Earth. So, there is a tug and a pull on the Earth, on this organism, and, I tell you, like all organisms, the Earth must react to its environment. And the environment for the Earth is vast and beyond your awareness. So, within the Earth and in the atmosphere of the Earth there is a churning. There is a moving. And it is as it is. Just as, my children, in your own bodies there is movement and churning. So it is in the Earth.

So, earthquakes will happen, as the Earth seeks balance within the larger system. Yes. And storms will rage because of the sweeping powers of the Earth in its environment. Yes. And so there is a web of cause and effect. Indeed. And I tell you, it is not the intention of the Earth to destroy. But the Earth as an organism must exist in a web of influences. So, there is tragedy. There is tragedy and the Holy weeps, the Holy weeps for the suffering and the loss. But finally, my children, there is restoration.

Now, there are some occurrences that happen in the Earth because of human action. Certainly. Human action is creating an imbalance within the system of causes and affects and influences. Therefore, the civilizations are indeed enhancing some of the powers of the storms and the heat of the planet. For I tell you, it is the heat of the planet that is often the foundational motion of storm. Civilization has very little effect upon earthquakes, my children. Some effect but very little. Weather patterns humanity can not consciously shape but the civilizations are causing variations in temperature because of a deterioration of atmosphere and pollution. So, the question finally is, should there be prayer, should there be prayer? Certainly. Prayer helps. Prayer helps all things. It helps the lives in the areas that are affected. It is the prayer of intervention. It is also possible to pray for the Earth and to help to place in balance the energies of the Earth.

So, yes, my daughter. Yes. Often the occurrences are indeed neutral. There is not intention in disaster. There is not intention through disaster in Earth or in Spirit. So, disaster is not placed upon a group to teach a lesson, as retribution. It is not so. It is not so. It is not so.

Embodied Spirit, my children, embodied Spirit is affected by the influences of the environment. It is a natural law, shall we say. A natural law.

## Our Bodies and the Earth

**Diane:** Can we talk about love in the Earth? I think from what I can understand and I'm not sure, I'd love this to be your feelings about this and your thinking about this. It seems that

Sophia is the bridge that opens the body to the Spirit and thus opens us up to love of the Spirit and love of the Earth. And is it, is it, is the love part, the more we love our own bodies and each other, is that in relationship to how the Earth is also being loved by the Spirit? Is it the same thing? Love must be the key here. Is it the key here? In the way we love the Earth? And is that why when we would love our bodies more and we would love the Earth more that we would act better towards the Earth and towards our bodies?

**The Messenger:** I shall provide a long yes to your question and provide perspective for what you sense and what you know, for the knowledge comes to you from the Spirit. It comes to you in your body, through your body, this awareness. So, my children, first of all, let us speak of the integration of your bodies and the Earth. For your bodies are made of Earth substance. And the Earth substance is made of star substance. And star substance is made of Holy substance. And Holy substance simply is.

So, at the very core of your physical being you are fundamentally related to the substance of the Earth. Therefore, the Earth speaks to your bodies, and your bodies respond to your natural environment. Such is the integration of Spirit, Body and Earth. So, one question is, does loving the body help one love the Earth? Shall I tell you, yes. Listening to the body allows one to listen to the Earth. So, those who learn to listen to their bodies learn to listen to the natural needs of their bodies; thus, their contemplations turn to the Earth. And they begin to become aware of what they take from the Earth, what they internalize from the Earth. It is the beginning of understanding and awareness.

Now, let us speak of love, let us speak indeed, my children, of love. Love. There should be many words to express the varieties of love. Let us speak of the love of the Holy. The love of the Holy is the love of giving of self in order for life to become. It is not only a sacrificial love, it is a love of generosity. It is a love without expectation, but it is a love that creates relationship. So, my children, to love without expectation is to say that you love without expecting a certain result. But love is always given with the intention of relationality, for love comes from the awareness that all things are related. So, the love of the Holy is a love of generosity. And the love of the Holy echoes through creation and is voiced in the Earth. So, the Earth has a love of generosity and abundance of self sacrifice. The love of the Earth gives for the wholeness and well being of all. And this, this is the love of the Holy. It is Holy love, my children. And you are capable of Holy love. So, the Earth resonates with Holy love. The cosmos resonates with Holy love. And you, my children, are products of Holy love. You are the products of the generosity of the Holy in the Earth. For when I say the Holy, I include the Earth. So let us not separate the Holy of the Cosmos from the Holy of the Earth. We shall simply say the Holy through the Earth.

So, my children, the Holy through the Earth exemplifies Holy love, a sacred love, and therefore expects relationship and awareness of relationality. And you have the capacity of sacred love, and if you were to love the Earth with sacred love and love each other with such a love and love yourselves with such a love, then the awareness of the Sacred would pervade all things that you do and you would understand that all things are related. What you do to the Earth, you do to all. What you do to your neighbor, you do to all. What you do to yourself, you do to all.

So, we come, then, to the awareness of the self which so often is the central origins of action. Those who know to love themselves also know to love others. These people understand how to love the Holy and the Holy in the Earth and through the Earth. So, love, indeed, my children, love, indeed, my daughter, is fundamental, fundamental to all of Creation. Love is the origin of all things, and love shall be the end of all things. And if love could be the foundation of all activity, then there would be balance and well being. Does this make sense to you?

## The Black Madonna

**Diane:** Yes. Could you speak about what we call the Black Madonna. There are many of us having dreams about her. She comes as a foreign body in our dreams, and she comes as a black woman, a dark woman, and she comes almost as a warning us to...to love better, to bring to light some of the love that we have for ourselves and for others. And I'm just wondering if many of us are dreaming of this dark mother, is this the warning you are saying to us about the Earth going into some kind of cataclysmic being in order for the balance to take place? Or is this just that many of us are becoming, realizing now that we have to bring to light the love on the Earth for ourselves and for the Earth and for each other?

**The Messenger:** You dream in ancient symbols, ancient symbols that you inherit from generations of experience. You have already spoken of Sophia. Now you speak of the Black Madonna. And there is a great deal to tell you about masculinity and femininity, but we shall leave this for another time. At the moment we shall focus upon the message of this Spirit of Wisdom that comes to you in the image of a dark woman. Often, the Spirit of Wisdom, which is the Spirit of Knowledge about Sacred relationship, is portrayed in the feminine. So, what comes to you, my daughter, in these dreams is the awareness of Sacred relationship coming to you as a dark woman. A dark woman which represents both the familiar and the unfamiliar. So, there is familiarity in the gender for you. There is familiarity in the message to you. But there is an unfamiliar element to this messenger, and therefore you must realize that the Holy is in both the familiar and the unfamiliar. So, the Black Madonna, as you call her, is appearing to the people. She is providing a message to the people. It is a message of Sacred love, shall we say, but it includes the Earth. It is often her message to include the Earth. Love for the Earth and love for each other, my children. The Earth is aware of the turning of imbalance. The Earth is indeed aware. And the wheels shall continue to turn. And what shall be crushed as the wheels turn, my children? What shall be crushed? And what shall endure? And what relationship shall emerge? It is the will of the Holy through the Earth for the relationships to be whole and balanced. And this is the message that is sent to you, sent to you from the generations before and for the generations to come: That love is in the familiar and the unfamiliar.

Does this mean that those of dark skin would dream of the white Madonna so that there would be familiarity and unfamiliarity? The white Madonna, my daughter, has already been imbued with multiple meanings. So, it may come as a different whiteness, an unworldliness. Indeed. So there is familiarity and unfamiliarity. So it is startling and new. Does this make sense to you?

**Diane:** Thank you very much. It does.

## Tracking

**The Messenger:** My daughter, Sandy, why do you not ask about tracking the animals?

**Sandy:** I was being polite and waiting my turn. But I think they're done. And besides, it's really emotional. So, I ask about tracking animals. I ask about our work with Coyote Trails and the way we teach tracking. I ask for confirmation on what we do well because I feel limited by time. I feel there is so much to do. And I want to spend my time doing what works. And I'm looking for guidance from Grandmother as to what have we done, Grandmother, that has made a difference? Grandmother, the Earth, what advice would you give to continue this work so we can renew that energy, that connection between the people who need to be connected to the Earth? It's all about tracking, I know it is. Somehow.

**Grandmother:** I would tell you, I would tell you, Granddaughter, that I see you. And I speak to you. And I hear you. And I hear many. And I speak to many. And you are not so few as you fear. You are not so few as you fear. For they are coming together, those who know how to speak to me. They gather, and they learn the languages so do not be afraid, my daughter. Do not be afraid. I speak to many who speak to me. In many different ways I speak. And I am always speaking even if the people do not listen, I speak. I speak. I speak.

So, is it discouraging to speak when I am not heard? It has always been the case that I am not heard. But lately I am indeed heard less often. It is, indeed, isolating. It is isolating. I put my energies and my concentration on those who hear. Those who listen.

My presence is for all people, but there is a flow that occurs when there is interaction. And flow increases flow and presence. I am more present to those who listen and speak. How else shall it be? Avenues are created. Avenues as strands, veins. And so the message comes through the strands. The message comes through the strands.

How do I speak to you? I speak through the creatures. I speak to you through the creatures. They listen to me. They listen to the turning and churning of me. And so your need cries out and I respond. And who, you might ask, am I? Who Am I? Who am I? I am the Holy. I am the Holy that moves through the Earth and gains consciousness of Earth. It is the same spirit, but my voice is different, the language is different. The message is the same. Be aware that the Holy message is the same, whether it comes from the cosmos, whether it comes from humanity, through humanity or whether it comes through the Earth, the message is the same. The people must learn how to love the messengers, the messengers of the Holy. And I am a messenger. And more than that, I am a giver of life. My message is for life. My message is for life. And when you see my language, my daughter, when you see, when you track down the signs, you are in relationship with me. You hear me. You see me. You feel me. And there is a relationship. There is a flow and a great joy, a great joy, a great joy.

See your tracking, then, as a way of reading my language, and when you track with concentration, you enter a trance with me, and we establish a deep, spiritual bond, you and I.

Why was there sorrow when you were tracking? Why was there sorrow coursing through you? There is also sorrow in the Earth. Sorrow in me. There is both joy and sorrow at the same time. Can you imagine, can you imagine, granddaughter, having many, many children? Having many children and let's say, can you imagine having a hundred children and they all go off and live their separate lives and then one returns? There is great joy, there is great joy in the meeting, but also great sorrow for the loss. Do you understand both at the same time?

**Sandy:** Yes, I do.

**Grandmother:** Joy and sorrow. Gain and loss. Therefore, see the Earth, see me as a Mother to many children, to many children who go their separate ways and forget their mother, forget their place of origin, forget that which sustains them and nurtures them, comforts them. There is sorrow and then there is great joy, great joy. And always there is the message, I am here, I am here, I am here, I am here. Always there is this message. In every breeze. In every season. And every bird chirp. And every dog bark. There is the message, I am here, I am here, I am here, I am here. In the very waters that flow is the message. It is everywhere. Everywhere. Learn the language, my daughter, and I shall speak. I shall speak. And I shall love. And you shall love.

**Sandy:** Thank you, Grandmother. I...Do you have any...I work with the children and at an age when they're beginning to forget. It's a transition time. Is there anything we could be doing differently or better to help them not forget as they go into adulthood?

**Grandmother:** Bring them into relationship. Bring them into relationship with the Spirit through the Earth, the Holy through the Earth. Let them read the signs. My granddaughter, you are all constructed to learn and know my language. You are all formed to know the language, so get them into the woods and they will hear me. They will feel me. And they will not forget. They will not forget. They will not forget. And know this. Know this. Know this. The power of the Earth is tangible in the natural environment. It is tangible in the natural environment. So, the people go to the wilderness, they go to the woods, they come to the waters to hear the Holy and this is good. This is good.

For I tell you, as the people live in the concrete of civilization, they forget. They forget. They forget. So, it is not a surprise that they shall come to the forest to rejuvenate their attachment to the Holy in the Earth, for they are surrounded by the Holy in the Earth in such places. They are surrounded by it. It envelopes them. So, there is communication. There is communication. So, my daughter, run to the woods and play with the children, and you will teach them the language of the Holy in the Earth. It is fundamental instruction. Fundamental human, spiritual instruction. The most fundamental that there is.

**Sandy:** I will do that. Grandmother, is there anything I can personally do for you?

**Grandmother:** It is love, it is simply love, it is simply love. It is simply love.

**Sandy:** Thank you.

## Living in Relationship

**The Messenger:** Grandmother, the Earth, loves you all, and her voice is a comfort, is it not? Are there other questions, my children? Other questions?

**Holly:** I have one more to follow the discussion with Sandy about the creatures, which is my big love, and the plants and the flowers and how we can best learn to communicate. You touched on that some, but how we can best learn to communicate through them. And is simply touching a flower in love effective to heal and spread love? How can we best communicate?

**The Messenger:** How can you best live in relationship? How can you best be an avenue for the sacred love to enter you and flow through you? Simply awaken awareness, awaken awareness of the Holy in all things. Certainly, touching a flower allows you to share the Holy energy. It allows for the energy to flow to and from. Yes, it is a sacred touch, a sacred touch. But you can also have a sacred exchange simply by opening to the Holy, opening awareness, opening your bodies to the Holy awareness that flows through nature, through all things. Once you know the Holy in nature you can feel the Holy in others, you can feel the Holy in all things. And once you know the Holy in others, you can feel the Holy in nature. There is no correct order in which to enhance awareness. It is simply opening to the awareness of the Sacred and knowing that you, your identity and yourself expands beyond the limits of self. And so you see your Self in all things, in nature. This is why it is fundamental to love your Self. For if you can love your Self, you can love your Self in all things, you can love the selfless Self.

So, on a larger scale, what can the people bring to Earth? What can the people bring? Certainly, they can bring awareness so as to change civilization. More than that they can bring their Holy presence to the Earth for the Holy courses through you also, my children. You are also generators. Yes, the Holy courses through you, so you can bring the Holy to the Earth. Does the Earth need such a small bit of Holy energy that you would bring? I tell you, the Earth absorbs it, and you become one with the Earth, and, therefore, the relationship to the Earth is restored. Because, my children, you are showing love. Love. Show love to the Earth and be loved. Show love to the Earth and live as the Earth would have you live, live as the Holy would have you live.

Love yourself. Love the Earth. Love each other.

What more is there to the Sacred rules of living? But we must be sure to add to those faiths that do not have the essential element; love the Earth. It is fundamental and it has been severed. So, love yourself. Love each other. Love the Earth. And live in balance and harmony. This is the fundamental Sacred teaching of all teachings. Love yourself. Love each other. Love the Earth. Be at peace and be whole. Be fulfilled.

**Diane:** I somehow feel that we have to ask forgiveness for all the centuries of...

**The Messenger:** Neglect.

**Diane:** Breaking a covenant. It feels like, before we can even do that, we have to acknowledge that we've broken covenants with the Earth, and I'm feeling that strongly today. Feeling that maybe we have to acknowledge what it is that we have done in the past in order to move forward to the future.

**The Messenger:** There's wisdom in your impulse. Wisdom in your desire. Wisdom in your plan. There is forgiveness in the Holy. There is forgiveness always. But there are times that human awareness must come to an acknowledgment of imbalance, misbehavior, misapplication of gifts and abilities. It brings a sense of humility and responsibility, and through humility and responsibility sacred awareness is awakened. So, my daughter, it is not a necessity to ask forgiveness from the Earth, but it may be a very honorable and productive activity. So, are there sacred gatherings that would say on behalf of humanity, we seek forgiveness? We seek forgiveness for growing away from the Earth, for neglecting our relationship to the Earth, for seeing only dead commodities in the Earth, and therefore taking and abusing and ignoring the Earth? Certainly, this can enhance the open awareness of the relationship between the human and the Earth and all of Creation. It is not a necessity, but it is an honorable and productive activity as a part of the awakening. For confession, my daughter, brings with it a sense of freedom. And with freedom comes the ability to live anew. So, live anew.

The energy is drawing to a close, my children. So be at peace and know that your work is Holy and know that the Earth listens and speaks. So, come to the Earth to hear the lessons. Come to the Earth to give your love and know that the lessons and the love of the Earth are given without expectation but through relationship.

**Diane:** Thank you. Thank you for touching our lives today and our hearts today in a special way.

**Voices:** Thank you.

**The Messenger:** Be at peace.

**Christopher:** Yes, you shower blessing upon this household and all our relations. Open the founts, open the veins and send the flow from the eternal to this time and from this time to the eternal. Let Holy flow to Holy, let our gesture open up a permanent connection that grows. That this day be multiplied.

**Sandy:** We are grateful for your love and we send our love to you. Please feel our love as well.

## CHAPTER 9

# Circles and Gatherings: The Spiritual Awareness of Our Time

*This lesson was received on April 25, 2010. The focus of the lesson is on the gatherings of spiritually-seeking people that are taking place around the world. These gatherings or circles are described as the greatest spiritual movement of our time. At the center of these gatherings is the yearning for the Holy, free from institutionalized dogma.*

MY CHILDREN, I see you. I see you. It is good to be among you. It is good to see you. It is good to complete the circle with you. For what is the circle without the Spirit? So, I shall come to represent the Spirit among you, the Spirit with you, the Spirit through you, the Spirit beyond you, the Spirit within you. And hence, we shall complete the circle: the circle of being, the circle of creation, the circle of existence. Indeed.

## The Circles and Gatherings

There is no circle without the Spirit for the Spirit is the thread that unites the elements into circularity. The Spirit is the substance that informs and transforms. The Spirit is the primary substance of existence, and yet it has no form. How can a substance have no form? How can a substance at the foundation of all being be formless? I tell you, the Spirit sweeps in energy, and in energy it is known, and through energy all things come. And so the formless shall take form in and through the energy that binds the elements.

So, let us speak of the form of transformation among the people, for transformation is taking place in the gatherings. Let us speak of the gatherings of the people. Let us speak of the renewed awareness of the Sacred, for this is what is coming to pass, my children. In your time the great gatherings are taking place. And in the gatherings there is renewed awareness. And in the renewed awareness there is great grace and acceptance and peace and love. It is the greatest movement humanity has ever known, and it takes place now in hidden places. It takes place now in full sight of the leaders and yet unknown to them. It takes place now amongst the people. And yet even these people are unaware of the linkages that are taking place. So, we shall name it into awareness.

We shall speak of circles. We shall speak of centerless circles. We shall speak of circles merging with circles. We shall speak of a centerless center. We shall speak of the emptiness of nothing that is all things. And we shall reveal that the people gather in centerless circles to share the Holy, and in these gatherings sacred awareness shall be renewed.

## The Spiritual Shift of Our Time

My children, there is a great emphasis on a new awareness that is coming upon the people. It is true that you are in a time of an immense spiritual shift, but I would not call it a new awareness. I would call it a RE-newed awareness. For the awareness is ancient; it is renewed in your time. The significance of this renewal is that it is collective. Never before has humanity come to a time of collective, universal awareness of unity and interdependence, and it is an awareness that is born of the Spirit. Where is this awareness taking form? In circles and gatherings of sacred intention.

Be aware, my children, that the circles are formed through sacred intention. It is the Spirit that binds the circles together.

So let us turn our attention to the gatherings, my children, to the gatherings, to the circles within circles.

## Being Centerless as Yearning for the Holy

My children, humanity has been knocked off center. Yes, humanity has been de-centered, shall we say. The center has been pulled out, and, my children, this is the greatest opportunity of the present age. Many panic because humanity is de-centered, and they clutch at an old center, an old answer, a single truth. But to be uncentered is to be alive, for at the center of all sacred gatherings and at the center of your being there is an emptiness. And it is as it should be. For I tell you, the universe begins in emptiness. It is the void. It is the expanse. It is the place of possibility. It is the origin of creation.

Allow me to explain the centerless center that is Sacred. At the center of sacred gatherings, there must be an emptiness, and this emptiness is the yearning for the Sacred. This emptiness cannot be filled, but it is the avenue for fulfillment. My children, the yearning for the Holy cannot be quenched. Indeed, the yearning for the Sacred grows stronger as you come closer to your own spiritual center. This yearning is an emptiness that is fulfilled but never filled. So, at the center of your life and at the center of your gatherings, there should be the emptiness of the sacred yearning. How shall you symbolize this sacred yearning? Do you see, the Sacred cannot be symbolized, epitomized, characterized, analyzed. The Sacred escapes all definitions. Thus, the Sacred shall be sought in the emptiness of all possibility.

And, my children, when this emptiness is filled, then humanity is lost, for suddenly fulfillment comes from something other than the Holy. So, there are people who walk about in their days filling their void with material, filling their void with work, filling their void with distraction. They are filling their void with belongings, filling their void with sorrow, filling their void with desire, filling their void as a way of avoiding the Holy yearning. My children, the void is not to be avoided. When you recognize the Holy emptiness as the Sacred, then you realize the emptiness must remain unfilled because the yearning for the Holy drives you. And I tell you, the Holy can not be captured. The Holy cannot be represented. The Holy cannot be understood. The Holy, indeed, is centerless, for at the center of the Holy Whole is the void of being.

How, then, can you fill the void? My children, you cannot. So, be centerless, my children. Be centerless, always aware that the Holy is your center and that the yearning for the Holy is your purpose and meaning and fulfillment. And if you can fill this emptiness, then you have not been receptive to the grandeur of the Holy. So, your center shall be empty and in the emptiness there is blessing.

Do you see? The Holy cannot be boxed in, and a new movement comes upon the people. It is a movement of circles gathered to share the Holy. For the way of the box has come to an end. The way of the box is revealed to be sterility. It is the way of the circles, of the many circles merging, converging, rippling out that is taking form among the people.

So, let us look to the gatherings, for the great power of the gatherings is this: They are centerless; therefore, they have been unrecognizable, for there is no doctrine at the center. There is no personality at the center. So, a great movement is sweeping among the people, unrecognized, unspoken, uncharacterized. The people are gathering in circles with a yearning for the Sacred, and they have rejected the singularity of the voices, shall we say, the centered voices. And they have instead come to understand that the many voices can ring true simultaneously. Therefore, my children, it is not only a circle without a center, it is a circle of many centers. Do you see? The centerless becomes the many centered.

## The Multi-centered Circles

So, how shall we have it that there is no center or that there are many centers? And is it not the same thing? To be centerless is to have many centers. And so I see circles gathering, people gathering to know the Holy, to experience the Holy, to share the Holy. And the circles begin to overlap, and the circles begin to align, and the circles begin to blend, and there is solidarity in these circles. But it is difficult to recognize for the circles are multi-centered and centerless. How, then, shall we recognize that they are seeking the same substance of Spirit? How does one name a centerless circle?

My children, the circles gather not to magnify a name or nation. The circles gather for the experience of sharing the Sacred. And the people yearn for the sharing. The people yearn for the Sacred, and they are expanding beyond the languages, the dogmas, the traditions. But they are not rejecting the old ways. They are also embracing them. This is the new awareness. It is indeed the new awareness of the Braided Way. One need not reject the old ways to be centerless. No. One can embrace the old ways and be multi-centered.

## The Breath of the Holy Bubbling from the Depths

So, my children, see in your mind's eye the center of *this* gathering, even here. See first that your gathering is centerless, that hunger for the Holy is at your center. The desire to be in contact with the Sacred, to be informed by the Sacred, to be transformed by the Sacred centers you, shall we say, unites you. But see, my children, that the centerless center begins to take form and there are multiple centers within this center.

See, my children, it is as if there are bubbles in the middle of your gathering. Many centers and each transparent. Shall we say they are as bubbles on the surface of the waters. And, my children, do you see they merge? Do you see they blend?

This is the great movement of your time. The gatherings have begun. The people come together to experience and know the Sacred. They come with an openness of the many ways forming one Way. And when these circles begin to overlap and blend, the renewed awareness of unification shall come to the people. It is indeed like bubbles on the surface of the deep, merging and blending by the breath of God.

My children, the Holy waters are at your center and the breath of God is blown into the waters. And behold, there are bubbles sprouting. This is the center that you shall seek, a center of Holy inspiration. The bubbles of Holy breath are at the center. And, my children, within these bubbles are many languages, many ways to understand the Holy, many ways to approach and experience the Sacred. And behold, my children, as you see these bubbles, you see not only the center of your circle, you see the many circles that are erupting on the surface of the deep. See, then, my children, the circles, the gatherings of the people. I tell you, I see these gatherings across the face of the Earth, and the gatherings are beginning to touch one another. And they are all Holy inspired, inspired by the wholeness. And this is the great movement of your time. The circles gather and blend and celebrate the diversity of holy experience.

And behold, perhaps the bubbles do not remain intact. Perhaps they pop and the breath returns to the Spirit, but it is not of great consequence for there are other circles being gathered. And so the groupings of people come together possibly for short periods, but the transformation of the Spirit is eternal. So, the circles may in fact fade, but the people are gathered up again into new circles of inspiration. These circles are inspired by the breath of God, and it is the breath of the Holy that gives them life.

So, the circles may be temporary, but they are also ancient, for they spring from a long line of inspired human awareness. So, then, look to the fundamental origins of the circles, and see that it is the breath of the Holy. It is indeed the breath of the Holy coming to you now through generations of experience. Coming to you now. Coming to you now.

## Gatherings for Sacred Experience

So, the gatherings call the people into the experience of the Sacred. And the gatherings shall allow the experience to spread. And through the common experience of the Sacred, a renewed awareness shall emerge. And in the renewed awareness there shall be acceptance and generosity. And through the acceptance and generosity, the unification shall be acknowledged. And the unification is not human centered. It is centerless. Therefore, it is Holy centered. And to be centered on the Holy is to be centered on all of the Holy's creation. So, through the centerless centers, through the gatherings of the people, through the sacred circles comes an awareness that the human is not the center of the universe but is connected to the Sacred through creation.

## Naming the Present Spiritual Movement

My children, it is the spiritual awareness of your generation. It comes in a time of great need, a time when the fabric of creation is worn thin. To facilitate transformation, the circles must be recognized and linked. Herein lies a great paradox, my children. For the centerless centers of the circles must be recognized and the movement must be seen.

Shall there be a prophet to rise up? Shall there be a spokesperson? Shall there be a center to this movement? I tell you, it is not to be. It is not to be. For, if there is a single voice, then the message of unification shall be distorted and finally corrupted. The Way of many ways would become the ONLY way, and humanity is again in a closed system.

So, we come to the conundrum: How to name the nameless. What shall you name the movement, my children? What shall you name it so that it can be recognize, but what name shall honor the multiplicities of centers?

You can not name it The Bubbles.

*[Laughter]*

You can name it the Centerless Circles. You can also name it the Braided Way. For the Braided Way is a framework to help you understand that the many ways intertwine into a Great Way.

For the time being, my children, it is necessary to name the movement so that it can be recognized. My children, you are given this awareness for a purpose, for the people need to know the movement takes place. So, you may name the movement the Braided Way or the Centerless Centers. But finally, the name is of no significance, for the gatherings shall not be about a language for the Sacred, they shall be about the experience of the Sacred. Yes, the gatherings shall be a way to celebrate the diversity of sacred experience.

Finally, all names shall fade, for the Ultimate Awareness is of the emptiness of being.

So, join a centerless circle and practice the Braided Way. Name it what you will, but engage in Sacred practice among the people, and know the unification of all things and all ways into the Holy Whole.

Are there questions?

## QUESTIONS AND ANSWERS

### Can the Circles Be Small?

**Sandy:** Is it important that these circles have many members? Can they be small circles?

**The Messenger:** Two or three are enough. The Holy is magnified in companionship. It is through community, through the gatherings that sacred awareness comes, for the awareness does not come to the isolated individual. No. The people are drawn to community because they are drawn by the Sacred into relationship. And this is the filament that holds the pieces of the circle together: Relationship. And the Spirit is the foundation of relationship. So, the people are drawn into relationship and it is through relationship that sacred awareness is inspired.

So, do not be a lone voice, my children. Be a circle. Be a gathering. And know that your gathering shall influence other gatherings. How shall this be, my children, but do you not know you are already a part of many gatherings?

So, this circle shall dissolve and the members shall disperse. And you shall be embraced by other circles. And through this embrace, this cross fertilization, the message is spread. Circle to circle. And then, my children, this circle comes together again but the elements are altered, are they not? So, the circle is altered. My children, do you see? Do you see? Spread yourself out among the peoples. Come to the Holy for sacred inspiration. Bring who you are and be changed and come back to your circle altered with new awareness and perception. This is the Holy way. It is the way of the Sacred. Transformation is invited, diversity is celebrated and awareness is expanded. Do you see, my children? The entire purpose of Creation is for expansion and celebration for possibility. And the circles are beginning to encourage possibility amongst the people. So, see that you are a holy family, my children. You, in this circle, are a holy family. And you shall send your members out into other circles so that when you come back you are transformed and the circle is expanded and your awareness is deepened. Do you see? Do you see?

The boundaries of religion are not important to these gatherings. The boundaries of nation are transgressed in these gatherings. The boundaries of class, the boundaries of gender, the boundaries of race and ethnicity all pass away in these gatherings, for the center is the hunger for the Holy. So, do not put in the center an idea of success, an idea of prosperity, an idea of nationality, an idea of religion, an idea of identity. No, leave it centerless so all ideas come to nothing but the Holy.

Does this make sense?

**Voices:** Yes.

## Bubble Bursting

**Diane:** So, if you look at me, I just came from a circle gathering at St. Peters community and my question is, it's an unrecognizable group, but we are being recognized by leadership and we are being excommunicated from a big circle, and it will cause a huge amount of conflict, and I feel like I'm in the middle of that conflict. And even though we're together as a group cinna I know that this is probably the Spirit's movement in it, the Holy's movement in it. I wonder if it is in my life right now? Is this where I'm supposed to be?

**The Messenger:** My daughter, you are a bubble burster.
*Laughter*

**The Messenger:** And I do not mean this in a negative way. The circles are in transformation for the people are being transformed. The gatherings with a defined center can no longer hold the transformed people. Do you see? So, the transformed people are bursting the barriers, spinning away from the center. And this is what you experience. So, this means that the center of the traditions are also being transformed, but the transformation shall take great time for institutions do not change quickly. They are not organic.

You may perceive that your church is being closed down by the institution; however, the closing is a part of a larger spiritual movement. The institution cannot evolve, so it is closing a church. Why? The attendance is low and the administration is stretched thin. Controversies abound. The people seek the Spirit elsewhere, or nowhere.

But here you are in other circles in addition to the church that is closing. You are following the Spirit, my daughter.

What is taking place is an evolution. Those things that can evolve are organic for they react to their environment. So, my daughter, you recognize the organic nature of the Holy, and you find yourself at the sight of bubble bursting. And here you are amongst the circles playing your role between the circles. And you have noticed that each circle invites a different language, a different framework of understanding. This awareness comes to the teachers of the Way. You must adapt. You must indeed adapt. This is why the Holy has brought a new terminology to this circle so you can speak of the Holy and the Sacred. You can speak of the Wholeness of the Sacred in ways that do not isolate but invite. Do you see?

**Diane:** I do. It causes a kind of homelessness, doesn't it, for the one who is in many circles?

**The Messenger:** Yes, indeed, my daughter, indeed. Indeed, indeed, it is a time of disorientation. But the ones who are disoriented, the ones who are centerless, the ones who are homeless are actually more oriented than those in the institutions, for you are seeing the evolution. So, you find yourself in the lonely way. The lonely way.

But my daughter, look amongst you. There are so many lonely ones. So, the lonely way becomes the holy way. And the gatherings of the lonely ones are the strongest gatherings of all. For in these gatherings the centerless nature is embraced, and the Holy inspires. So, gather the lonely ones. Gather the lonely ones, my daughter, out of a yearning for the Sacred. So the lonely way is not the only way, my daughter. No, the lonely way invites new circles to be established outside of the center of the institution.

**Diane:** I love the people that are in my old circles, though, and I feel a rupture of relationships. And I don't want that to happen. I know it can't go both ways. I know I have to keep speaking the truth, but I feel that the breaking off of relationship, all relationships, and I try to find a way to keep those relationships intact. And I think my question is, will they be able to stay intact when the circles are disbanding or when I'm being literally excommunicated from one circle?

**The Messenger:** It is a time of upheaval, is it not?

**Diane:** It is.

**The Messenger:** Which causes panic amongst the people and pain and sorrow and grief. Relationships alter and change. They must, and so you are in the midst of the alteration. My daughter, you are in the midst of a time of evolution. The organism is changing. So, we shall look at these bubbles as cells. The cells of the organism are changing. You are being regrouped and re-gathered. How, then, do you honor the relationships of the centered circles, of the disbanded circles? The relationships are of the Holy and these relationships will endure. They will endure if they are recognized as holy relationships. And recognition, my daughter, is a primary concern. For there are times that you can recognize the holy ties when others cannot. And when the ties are not recognized they become threadbare.

So, when you are excommunicated, my daughter, you are no longer recognized. Is this not so? Because of the changing of circumstances. But you may be able to recognize the holy ties for the Holy is eternal despite circumstances. So, my daughter, you are called to honor the relationships, to recognize them, but do not be surprised if recognition does not come back to you. And this shall cause great sorrow and grief in you and in the Holy. But there is celebration in the new ties that are being formed, the new awareness that is being transformed. Does this make sense to you?

**Diane:** It does and it's already there. Joy is there. Thank you.

## Decentered Times

**The Messenger:** I tell you, it is not right to be dismissive of the old circles and institutions for they are a source of great wisdom. And it is through these circles, through the traditions that the teachers will rise. It is merely a new awareness that must come upon the people, an awareness that sees the validity of the many circles. And the center that must come out of the established circles is the center of exclusivity which is a center of certainty. Do you see? Ambiguity must come to the center, the ambiguity of the Holy. The Holy cannot be known. Take out this center and the circles ironically grow stronger for your time is a decentered time, my children. For if the human is the center of your perspective, then all things are out of balance. Remove yourselves from the center. Put instead the Holy in the center and there shall be balance. Remove the illusion of control from the center and instead put the Holy in the center. Do you see, my children? Do you see? The institutions shall remain, but shall be decentered and the ones that cannot be decentered will crumble. This is ironic for you would think that if you take a system of thought and take the center of the system away then all things shall fall asunder. But the Holy works in reverse. Decenter the system and the system shall live, for at the center shall be the Holy. The Holy, the beautiful emptiness that is at once nothing and everything.

Take your concepts, my children, to the ceneterless center and drop them into the void. Drop them into the void.

Let go of your sense of identity, your sense of control, your sense of success, your sense of achievement, your sense of self. Drop them into the void, and see a new creation coming forth. A new creation. A life centered on the beautiful emptiness of the Holy. It is a great call among the people. And when you see that the Holy is the center, then all things come into perspective, and you see that all of creation is equally important, and then there is balance and wholeness. Does this make sense?

**Voices:** Yes. Yes it does.

**The Messenger:** Be decentered. Be knocked empty, and there shall be life. It is not destruction. It is not deconstruction. It is a flowering of sacred awareness. It is the call of your times.

## Building Circles

**Sandy:** So, everything that you're saying strikes me very clearly. I see it. And I look at the circles that I play in now, and I love to build circles, I love to participate in circles, and I love to leave circles. What do I need to change? What do I need to do to go out, as you say, that is different than what I'm doing now to help this take place?

**The Messenger:** My daughter, you are a circle builder. A circle builder. It is easier to build new circles with the Holy in the center than it is to go into an institution and knock the center out. It is possible to transform the center of an institution, but it is easier to form a new circle with an awareness that there are other circles. So, this is what you do, my daughter, you build circles that overlap other circles. Intentionally. So, you work well in a good and Holy way.

**Sandy:** I have been playing around with the idea this last week, feeling pulled again for the first time in a long time to go back and I mentioned it to Jen. I want to play with the youth group within the institution. Thinking about going back in a little bit, in a very general way, a very unthreatening way, and I'm trusting that if the opportunity is presented and a new circle is built, and I intertwine those two things that all I have to do is just bring the people to the Earth. I don't have to organize them just create that soft structure and the Holy and the Sacred and the Earth will take care of the rest and let it happen on its own. Is that a good format or do we need, do I need to be stepping out stronger? You were very strong in your statement that we will go out, so any direction that you have for me personally or this group would be good.

**The Messenger:** To form a centerless center one must face the difficulty of representing the indefinable while allowing the mystery to remain a mystery. So, one can do this through the Earth for the mystery of the Erath is inviting. One can do this through the cosmos. One can do this through the Holy, for the Holy is the mystery. Let us gather around this mystery and experience the Sacred. And let us experience the Sacred in different ways. Celebrate the variety. The Earth is a mystery. Let us experience the Sacred in this mystery, and let us name our experiences and celebrate the variety and see that in the multiplicity there is indeed similarity. So, my daughter, to work in the centerless center one must be able to see the design of the Sacred. You must be able to name it quickly so the people can see. I speak in a different experience and yet there is a similarity for we come to the mystery together. I see your work, my daughter. It is good and noble Holy work.

**Sandy:** But there's more. I mean I feel like I'm getting ready for something I don't know I'm getting ready for.

**The Messenger:** Then be ready. Be ready.

**Sandy:** I think I understand centerless circles but what I haven't really hit me so strongly before is the beauty of…how do I say this? In the past before this world, before we became so tied economically, before the internet, before we became one world, one planet so tied together in so many ways, we were isolated. And in our isolated villages and countries and spaces we could have an individual rise up. And that individual could lead that group of people and provide enlightenment and guidance. But now because we are so tied so tightly as a world, one doesn't cut it anymore because it's yours, not mine. And it seems like your messiah wouldn't be my messiah and not only that but we could fight over it so easily now and compare so easily now. So when you say and when you talk about the centerless circle and about the Sacred and the mystery of the Sacred, it seems to me, it is just hitting me very strongly, of course, it's the only way we can bring the people together is to go back to the basic mystery, and we can all come and gather in a circle and we can all say together, yes, this is what we do not understand. So we are no longer fighting over who's right, who's wrong or whose messiah's better, but let's join together in what we do *not* understand. Is that reflected back right?

**The Messenger:** It is a good summation. It is a very good summation. It is indeed. I would add that if the movement were to have a singular voice, any singular voice would misconstrue from a singular language and a singular perspective. And then there would be a singular answer and a singular explanation. The time of singularity has come to a close amongst the people, so it shall be a time of braiding together the strands into the Whole with the priority on the Whole. So, the savior for this nation and the messiah for that nation and the name of the Holy for this group and the ceremony for sacred initiation in that group shall be embraced as all partial and beautiful fulfillments, experiences and manifestations of the sacred mystery. And soon the braid will begin to speak to the people. The braid itself will begin to speak and offer priorities. And offer practices. And offer inspiration and offer direction. Soon the braid will speak. The braid will speak.

So it is a holy, holy movement, and the one whom I possess (Michael) wonders what part to play in the holy movement. For he sees it. What part shall he play in the holy movement? His role is to be the messenger, to be the messenger. And the message has been sent. The question is how to communicate the message. And this is the work of his life. It is holy work. holy work.

Why doesn't it come in a more streamlined, efficient, communicative, marketable manner? We must work with the materials we are given. This, my children, is the nature of the communication. This is how it comes. So, it has been through the ages and so it shall be. This is how the enlightenment is explained. Circuitious, you might say. Indirect, you might say. Obtuse, you might say. Distill this, my children, distill it, and you will have poetry and paradox.

How, shall the people then approach the material? How shall it be communicated? It needs to be experienced. The Braided Way is a way of sacred experience.

My children, we come to a close. Michael's energy is waning, and the connection is drawn thin.

**Sandy:** Thank you for your presence. And thank you for your loyalty to us and to this task. You are always here when we call.

**The Messenger:** Indeed. It is the way of the Holy. The messengers, the healers, the companions are always present, waiting to be engaged in relationship. It is right to be thankful. It is right to be humbled. It is right to be drawn into holy relationship. You bless me, my children. You bless me with your questions and your open hearts. There is fulfillment in the Holy which is dependent on the openness of the human. The fulfillment is mutual, my children, and I am humbled and grateful, as well. Yes. It is a mutual fulfillment, so the blessings flow in circular motions from the eternal to the temporal, from the seen to the unseen, from the phenomenal to the spiritual. It is a beautiful circle to behold, for I see the blessings as light. Be, then, encircled in the Light of lights, my children, and the blessings shall flow. Let the blessings flow. Let the blessings flow. In, through, and beyond this circle. In, through, and beyond your Selves. Let the blessings flow.

# Acknowledgments

Fిఇఅఈసఄ, I GIVE DEEP GRATITUDE to the Holy, who has guided me in every step of the process of both life and the writing of this book. The Spirit of the Holy has been my companion, teacher, friend, and inspiration. I also want to acknowledge my friends in the "book group," who met together with me monthly to receive the material in this book: Chris Reynolds, Diane Pinchot, Holly Matson, John Davis, Kelly Cochran Davis, Jason Imbrogno, Jennifer Olin-Hitt, and Michael Durbin. I am especially grateful to Sandy Willmore, who organized the book group sessions and transcribed the recordings. Without Sandy this book would not have been written. Donna Wert was an enormous help in her edits and suggestions to improve the flow of the manuscript, and Sarah Adkins also gave wise editorial advice. It is a tremendous blessing to have my father, Terry Hitt, do the cover art for the book. I also have deep appreciation for Vanita Oelschlager for reading the manuscript and offering encouragement.